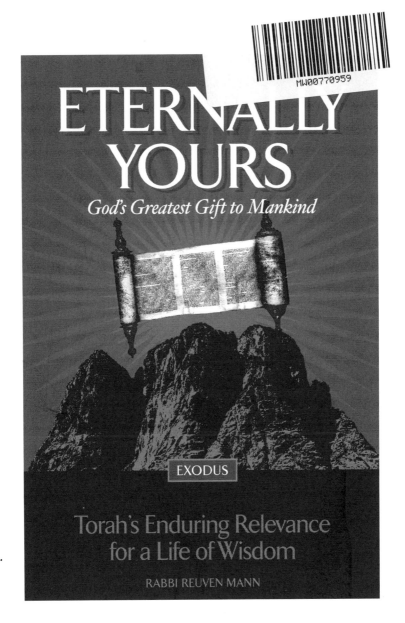

ETERNALLY YOURS

God's Greatest Gift to Mankind

EXODUS

Torah's Enduring Relevance for a Life of Wisdom

RABBI REUVEN MANN

Copyright © 2017 Reuven Mann
Published by: Observant Artist Community Circle, Inc.
All rights reserved.
ISBN-10: 0692991328
ISBN-13: 978-0692991329

DEDICATION

This book is dedicated to Jules Glogower, Yehudah ben Yehoshua Halevi, zichrono livracha, a modest and honest individual who was very meticulous in his tefillot. A clinical psychologist, blessed with deep insights into the human personality, he was a wise and loving adviser to family, friends and those in need. He faced life's challenges with humor, a calm disposition and clarity of thought. May his memory continue to inspire all who knew him.

In loving memory, The Glogower family

DEDICATION

This book is also dedicated to the memory of our parents:

Yetta and Harry Mann Z"L who always emphasized, by word and deed, the supreme importance of learning Torah, getting a good education and being a good Jew.

Sari and Herman Jacob Z"L who emerged from the concentration camps to rebuild their lives, raise a family and renew their dedication to Judaism, Israel and the Jewish People.

In loving memory,
Rabbi and Rebbetzin Reuven Mann

ACKNOWLEDGEMENTS

The articles in this book were written over the course of the last eight years. I began writing a weekly piece on the Parsha when I began my tenure as Rabbi of the Young Israel of Phoenix, Arizona. I would like to thank Maxine Blecher who was the shul Secretary for her assistance in this endeavor. At that time (before I became a user of the IPad) I wrote the articles in longhand and she was able to read them and type them up. We reviewed each column and her feedback contributed to the quality of the writing.

About four and a half years ago Devora Krischer, who had been a professional editor for Jewish publications, volunteered to perform that service for me. She had the essential qualification of being able to read my handwriting but more importantly applied her great editing skills to my compositions. Her insights and suggestions proved to be a great asset in enhancing the literary quality of my work.

Devora is a kind, caring and devoted woman who is always there to be helpful and contribute her substantial skills to the needs of the Jewish community. She continues to review and edit my weekly Torah essays with her characteristic enthusiasm and good cheer. I thank her and wish her good health and all of Hashem's blessings for many, many years.

This book is the brainchild of my student, Rabbi Richard Borah, who thought it would be a good idea to collect my Dvar Torah's and present them as a book for the Jewish and general public. He put in a great deal of work discharging the many tasks necessary to organize the publication of a book. He is himself the author of two works, "Man as Prime Mover: A Torah Perspective On Contemporary Philosophy and Science" and "The Rambam & The Rav On The 54 Portions Of The Torah".

I have greatly enjoyed our friendship and intellectual relationship which goes back a long way. I wish him and his wife Andrea great happiness and nachas from their beautiful children as well as Hashem's blessings in all that they do.

Another Talmid of mine, Rabbi Marshal Gisser, contributed his formidable skills to this book. He is an extremely talented graphic artist who is responsible for the front and back covers. I believe that Torah should be presented in a manner that is beautiful in both form and content. The aesthetics of a Sefer are important to me and Rabbi Gisser's work enabled that aspect of the work to be very appealing. His life is dedicated to the dissemination of Torah which he does via his writings on his website, Mesora.org. This resource provides great Torah teachings of Rabbi Gisser and numerous other Rabbis and reaches thousands of people many of whom have been brought closer to Judaism as a result. May Rabbi Gisser continue to advance in his study and teaching of Torah and merit Hashem's blessings in all his endeavors.

Finally, I would like to acknowledge the unique role my wife Linda has played in my life. Without her I could not have spent my time immersed in learning, teaching and providing guidance and counseling to individuals and married couples. Being Menahel of Yeshiva B'nei Torah as well as a community Rabbi consumed virtually all of my time. In addition students and congregants were a regular feature of Shabbat and Yom Tov meals and due to Linda's great cooking and hosting skills our home became the "invitation" of choice.

Linda is a very wise, determined, and capable woman whose dedication to our life's mission of disseminating Torah was absolutely vital to any success we achieved. Whoever feels gratitude to me for any way in which I benefited them must be equally thankful to her for she made it all possible. May she be blessed with good health and long years, nachas from children and grandchildren and her dream of spending much more time in Eretz Yisrael.

Table of Contents

Introduction

My entire career which spans over forty years has been dedicated to the dissemination of Torah Judaism in the settings of the classroom, Beit Midrash and Synagogue. As a Rebbe I have taught a number of subjects including Talmud, Chumash, Tanach and Hashkafa. My objective as a teacher was to penetrate to the depths of the classical Jewish texts (to the best of my abilities) and demonstrate how the ideas of Torah are Divine and therefore timeless and relevant to all of life's challenges.

My style of teaching was *not* to deliver lectures to my students. My classes are best described as *interactive.* I would generate a *participatory* analysis of the subject matter and encourage my students to ask the pertinent questions and try their hands at formulating meaningful answers. My goal was not to merely communicate information and concepts but to train the students to internalize the unique methodology which would enable them to become Torah scholars in their own right.

Through the years a particular love and fascination of mine was the study of Chumash. The subject matter therein is often presented in a *cryptic* manner. The profound ideas embedded in the narratives and other sections of the Chumash lie hidden beneath the surface and, just as in Talmud, one must learn to navigate it's "stormy seas" and extract its "buried" treasures.

Rabbi Chanina said (Taanis 7a), "I have learned much from my teachers, more from my colleagues and most of all from my students." I have been fortunate to learn from wonderful teachers. In addition to the great Roshei Yeshiva who taught at the Rabbi Isaac Elchanon Theological Seminary (Yeshiva University) during the 1960s, I also had the privilege to hear magnificent shiurim from the master, Moreinu Hagaon Rav Yosef Soloveitchik ZT"L. He was a genius of towering proportions in *all* areas of Torah knowledge whose ability to elucidate complicated ideas in the clearest and most compelling manner was legendary.

When I was a student "sitting at the feet" of these great Torah scholars my goal was not just to understand and absorb the content of what they were teaching. I also sought to understand their method of thinking and the special approach which enabled them to reach their brilliant conclusions. I was most focused on incorporating their *derech of learning* and developed a technique which I call "listening with the third ear" (borrowed from the title of a book by the famous psychoanalyst Theodore Reik). This enabled me to observe their thinking patterns and study how they would maneuver through the complicated material and arrive at their penetrating halachic formulations.

I also had the good fortune to meet and become close friends with Rav Yisrael Chait, Shlita. He was a student of the Rav whom I regard as a great intellect and master of the *Brisker Derech*. We would learn *bechavruta* (learning partners) and these sessions provided a great opportunity to advance my understanding and application of the Brisker approach.

In 1971 Rabbi Chait and I established Yeshiva B'nei Torah where I served as Menahel and Maggid Shiur for almost forty years. The intellectual atmosphere in this great place was intense and unique. I was always surrounded by formidable talmidim who had a seemingly insatiable desire for knowledge and understanding and were trained and encouraged to ask the most daunting questions.

A great benefit of being in the Yeshiva was the opportunity it provided to hear the special shiurim in Chumash given by Rabbi Chait. These were masterpieces of analysis and conceptualization of the Bible narratives. He would take apart a *sugya* and analyze the pertinent Midrashim and commentaries in order to flesh out the deeper ideas of the stories. He delivered *breakthrough* discourses on numerous areas such as "The Sin of Adam", "The Generation of the Flood" and that of "The Dispersion", "Yosef and His Brothers" and many others. Rabbi Chait was able to derive the philosophical principles that were at the heart of the Biblical stories and demonstrated how we can extract fundamental ideas relevant to all areas of life by a proper understanding of the Chumash.

Many of the ideas and approaches I incorporated in the following essays were inspired by elucidations I heard from Rabbi Chait. His influence can be seen in many places but most specifically in *No Good Deed Goes Unpunished, The True Test of Piety* and *Never Despair.*

I take this opportunity to express to him my great gratitude for all his friendship, teaching, personal advice and assistance in so many areas over the years. May Hashem grant him good health and strength to be able to continue his masterful teaching and personal guidance to all who seek it, for many, many years.

I have tried to utilize the approach outlined above in all of the many Chumash classes I have given over the years. I have taught male students at Yeshiva B'nei Torah, female students at Masoret: Institute of Advanced Judaic Studies for Women (which I and Rabbi Daniel Rosenthal founded in 1993) and to men and women at the various Synagogues at which I served as Rabbi, over the years (they include: Jewish Community Center of Inwood, Rinat Yisrael Of Plainview N.Y. and Young Israel of Phoenix, Arizona).

Most of the ideas contained in this book were worked out in creative sessions with the intellectually energetic students I have been fortunate to have. For the past eight years I have written a weekly column on the Parsha of the week. A student of mine Rabbi Richard Borah suggested that we organize these writings and compile them in a book for the benefit of others who might find them useful and interesting. Rabbi Borah has been a great help in the many tasks that must be accomplished before a book can "see the light of day."

I have utilized the classical sources such as the Midrashim, Rashi, Rambam, Ramban, Sforno, Ibn Ezra, Ralbag, Abarbanel, Malbim, Rabbi Samson Raphael Hirsch, Rabbi Yosef Soloveitchik and many others. My goal was not to merely repeat what they say but to analyze, clarify and make sense of their words and show how they enable us to elucidate the text.

It is my hope that this book will enhance the readers enjoyment and appreciation of Torah. I believe it will be of interest to the "ordinary" reader as well as teachers and pulpit Rabbis because it will stimulate thought and provide ideas and interpretations that will be worthy of analysis and discussion.

My greatest hope is that it will engender interest in and enjoyment of the study of Torah. I have referred to Torah, in the subtitle, as "Gods' greatest gift to mankind." It is unfortunate that many Jews do not look at it that way. It is my prayer that this work will make a contribution, however modest, to rectifying that situation.

Rabbi Reuven Mann, November 2017

Shemot

No Good Deed Goes Unpunished

The Book of Shemot describes the enslavement of the Jews and their transformation into a "kingdom of Priests and a Holy Nation." It's hard to comprehend how the offspring of Yaakov and Yosef could be so ill-treated by the Egyptians. Enumerating the factors that led to the slavery, the Torah states:

> A new king arose over Egypt, who did not know about Yosef. (Shemot, 1:8)

It is interesting to note that not everyone takes this statement literally. A great Talmudic Sage learns that this is a reference to the old Pharaoh, who adopted a "new" attitude (Rashi, Shemot: 1:8). At first glance, the notion that the Pharaoh whose dreams Yosef had interpreted was the one who initiated the oppression, is mind boggling. Are we to believe that the King who elevated Yosef to the most exalted position in Egypt, and enthusiastically welcomed his father and brothers to reside in the land's choicest location, would seek to crush their descendants in such a cruel manner? Unfortunately, we must answer in the affirmative and seek to learn the lessons contained in this interpretation.

One of the least attractive human character traits is the inability to appreciate the favors of others. The worst expression of this flaw is when someone repays a kindness with evil. We have all experienced this on some level. Sometimes we go out of our way and make an enormous sacrifice to benefit someone. However, a really big favor can spell the end of a friendship. The recipient of our kindness may not only fail to be appreciative, but might even resent and turn against us.

Jewish history illustrates the popular saying that "no good deed ever goes unpunished." Many kings have invited the Jews into their countries and granted them special privileges in order to profit from their commercial and other talents. Over time the economic prosperity the Jews engendered aroused envy and led to persecution and even expulsion. This pattern has been repeated many times. We were banished from England, Spain and other lands that gained greatly from the Jewish presence.

The most egregious example of this phenomenon is the case of Germany. Hitler accused the Jews of being a fifth column and "stabbing Germany in the back." Yet no group was as loyal to the country and contributed more to its economic, scientific and cultural advancement than the Jews. Will it be different in America? Jews have participated extensively in the civil rights struggles of persecuted peoples. As animosity toward Israel increases, it will be interesting to see whether these groups will join us in solidarity with the Jewish State.

The rabbi who learned that the "new" King was actually the old Pharaoh formulated a compelling insight into the deeper recesses of the human psyche. He was urging us not to put our faith in man, whose vanity and selfishness is boundless.

When Pharaoh needed Yosef he gave him great power and opened the land to his family. However, Pharaoh was incapable of genuine gratitude, for he regarded himself as a deity. It was a blow to his pride to be dependent on a Jew for survival. As the calamity of the famine receded, Pharaoh began to downplay the magnitude of Yosef's achievements. The Jews were a reminder of a dark period in his history, which he needed to forget.

Engaging in what psychologists call "reaction formation," Pharaoh viewed the Jews as enemies of the state, who must be subdued. There is much we can learn from this as individuals and as a people. Compassion must be practiced with wisdom and *restraint*. Let us never assume that our good deeds will be appreciated or bring us special favor. We should perform kindness and righteousness for its own sake, without any expectation of gratitude, and with full confidence that the ultimate reward is from Hashem.

Betrayal

A major theme in *parshat* Shemot is the development of the Jews from a small family of seventy members to a full-fledged nation charged with a Divine mission. The Jews are to be a "Kingdom of Priests and a Holy Nation" (Shemot: 19:6). At first glance, the description of the Jews as a kingdom of "priests" (*Kohanim*) is difficult to comprehend. Only a small group of people, a subdivision of the tribe of Levi, were designated as *Kohanim*, and tasked to perform the sacrificial service in the Temple. The right to bring sacrifices was exclusive as the Torah makes it clear that the "stranger [a non-*Kohein*] who draws near shall be put to death." (Bamidbar, 18:7) Why, then, are the Jews called a "Kingdom of Priests," if only a select few are actually priests? If that is the case, why is the *entire* nation referred to as "a kingdom of priests?"

The great commentator Sforno tackles this problem. He says that ministering in the Temple was not the primary purpose of the *Kohanim*. Rather, their mission was delineated by Moshe in his final blessings to the tribes. Regarding the tribe of Levi, he said:

> They shall teach Your ordinances to Yaakov, and Your Torah to Yisrael; they shall place incense before You, and burnt offerings upon Your altar. (Devarim, 33:10)

The basic role of the *Kohein* is to study and teach Torah to the Jewish people. His right to perform the sacrificial service stems from this total commitment to the study and teaching of Torah. It is *only* with regard to the Temple service that the Torah proscribes a "stranger" from approaching. However, when it comes to the "crown" of Torah (i.e., the right to study and teach it), Judaism is a complete democracy; *Kohanim* are no better than any other Jew.

Whoever obtains Torah knowledge, even if he is the most humble person, will be more respected than the mightiest king. It is in this sense that the Jewish people are characterized as a "Kingdom of

Priests," a nation of teachers whose task is to educate mankind to know the true God and to serve Him by emulating His ways of kindness and justice, which He has revealed in His Torah. It is for this purpose that the descendants of the patriarchs were transformed into a nation in the land of Egypt.

Betrayal-Part 2: Why Was Enslavement Necessary?

The parsha gives some insight into how this goal of becoming a special nation was achieved. The story begins with a monumental betrayal. Initially, the Jews had been welcomed to reside in Egypt by Pharaoh. Pharaoh's great gratitude to Yosef, and appreciation of his almost superhuman genius in shepherding Egypt through the years of famine that ravaged the world, carried over to Yosef's father and brothers. Indeed, the nation of Egypt mourned Yaakov's death for seventy days and a delegation of its most distinguished people accompanied the funeral procession all the way to Canaan.

But the Torah points out in the opening verses of Shemot that the high regard in which the Jews were held did not endure. As long as there were living reminders of all that Yosef had done, the Jews enjoyed peace. That situation was undermined when "Yosef and all his brothers and that entire generation died."(Shemot 1:6) As if this wasn't enough, there "arose a *new* king over Egypt who did not know Yosef." (Shemot 1:8)

The new king's attitude toward the Jews was that they were a disloyal people who wanted to take over the country and drive the Egyptians out. There was absolutely no basis for this claim. Indeed, the exact opposite was true. The Jews were responsible for saving Egypt from a famine that would surely have destroyed the country.

The cruel enslavement of the Jewish people and the slander of her character contain important lessons for us. The Rabbis say, "It is a *halacha* (natural law), Eisav hates Yaakov." The antipathy to Jews and Judaism is built into the scheme of things.

That is why all the major empires inevitably clashed with the Jews and sought their destruction. As Bilaam stated upon beholding *Bnei Yisrael* (the Jewish people), "they are a people that dwells apart and cannot be counted among the nations" (Bamidbar, 23:9).

We should seek to understand why it was necessary for the Jews to experience the betrayal and cruelty of the Egyptians. Perhaps the problem was that the Jews had become too comfortable and complacent, and trusted the Egyptians to maintain their security. Their dependency on Egypt had to be broken. Therefore, salvation came only when they "cried out to Hashem from the labor" (Shemot: 2:23). The Jews needed to disassociate themselves mentally and psychologically from reliance on the Egyptians. Only then could they obtain the proper relationship with Hashem as the exclusive source of their physical well-being and spiritual fulfillment.

In order to become a "Kingdom of Priests," we have to recognize the total moral bankruptcy of the nations, and the great need they have to be "instructed of the Lord." Jews must affirm the superiority of the Torah way of life, and practice it in a manner that enables us to be "a light unto the nations."

A Light Unto Ourselves

The entire purpose of man is to know his Creator and to seek perfection by emulating His ways. One might ask, "How am I to discover those 'ways,' and how can I internalize them?" The answer is Divine Revelation.

When Hashem charged Moshe with the task of leading the Jews out of Egypt, he wondered: By what merit did they deserve such Divine intervention? Hashem replied that the Jews were destined to receive the Torah on Mount Sinai. He would "personally appear" and reveal Himself to an entire nation to communicate the Ten "Commandments." The rest of the Torah would be revealed to His chosen prophet, Moshe, who would then transmit it to the Jewish people. The Jews are, thus, God's chosen people. The Creator of the universe selected us from all the nations to preserve His Torah way of life and to teach its fundamental ideas to mankind.

Have we succeeded in our national obligation? Has the promise made to Avraham, that "through you all the nations of the world will be blessed," been fulfilled? My own answer would be that we have achieved our goal to a *certain* extent. We have proclaimed the folly of idolatry and that the Deity is One, a true unity, beside Whom there is no other. In addition, the concept of universal human rights can be traced to the Torah. Judaism affirmed the dignity of mankind by asserting that all people have been created in the "Image of God." We are unequivocally opposed to any and all forms of prejudice based on gender, race, or color.

Christianity and Islam have attempted to convince the world that *they* are the source of the moral heritage of mankind. This is absolutely false. Let us take the virtue of compassion: that one should be concerned about and alleviate the suffering of others. There is no doubt in my mind that Judaism transmitted this teaching to the world through the compassionate lifestyle of our Patriarchs along with the exhortations of the Torah and subsequent prophets. The key verse adjuring us to merciful and benevolent behavior is in Vayikra:

> You shall love your friend as yourself. I am the Lord. (Vayikra, 19:18)

During one of my talks at Phoenix College, I asked a group of non-Jewish students: "Which religion teaches that you must love your neighbor as yourself?" They all responded, "Christianity." I then opened the Torah to the relevant verse in Vayikra and asked one of the students to read it aloud. The group was amazed to discover that something they had been taught as a classic Christian ideal was really from the "Jewish Bible."

We must be honest and admit that we have a long way to go before we can say that we have fulfilled our calling to be "a light unto the nations." We live in a world that is not breaking down our doors to hear our message. Nevertheless, we should not put the blame solely on the "nations." Before we can become a light unto others, we must be a light *unto ourselves.*

The latest studies show an alarming abandonment of Judaism by a significant majority of American Jews: Fewer than 10% identify with our religion and actively observe it. How can we expect non-Jews to live according to the moral imperatives of Judaism when the Jews themselves do not take the Torah seriously?

Throughout our history, we have been subjected to virtually every form of persecution. It began with the Pharaoh who falsely accused the Jews of being a "fifth column" who would turn against Egypt in its moment of vulnerability. The Egyptians sought to weaken the Jews by imposing harsh labor on them. However, as the Torah states:

> But as much as they would afflict them, so did they multiply and so did they gain strength, and they were disgusted because of the children of Israel. (Shemot, 1:12)

The irony of Jewish history is that affliction and persecution have made us spiritually stronger. In fact, anti-Semitism has played an almost indispensable role in preserving the identity of the Jewish people. The greatest spiritual threat we have ever faced is the complete freedom and acceptance offered by America. At the lowest moment of the enslavement in Egypt, Hashem sent Moshe to liberate the Jews both physically and spiritually. In America today, we are physically liberated, but spiritually endangered. We are very grateful to this country for all the freedom it has afforded us. Is it worth the spiritual cost at which it comes?

It is my fervent hope that the Jewish people will rediscover the hidden treasures of the Torah and recognize the universal value of our religious teachings. Then we will become a light unto ourselves and to the nations as well.

Va'eira

When Things Go South

In parshat Va'eira, the confrontation between Moshe and Pharaoh begins in earnest. Moshe's original engagement with Pharaoh had ended in disaster. Instead of gaining a hearing for the grievances of the Jews, his intercession made things worse. Pharaoh had increased the workload by making the Jews responsible for collecting the straw needed to make bricks. In spite of this new task, they were still bound to produce the same quota as before.

> You shall not continue to give stubble to the people to make the bricks like yesterday and the day before yesterday. Let them go and gather stubble for themselves.
>
> But the number of bricks they have been making yesterday and the day before yesterday you shall impose upon them; you shall not reduce it, for they are lax. Therefore they cry out, saying, "Let us go and sacrifice to our God." (Shemot 5, 7-8)

This situation put the Jews in an impossible position, and they lashed out at Moshe and Aharon. Moshe held himself responsible for this setback and complained to Hashem that "from the time I went to Pharaoh, things have worsened for the people." (Shemot 5:22)

Hashem responded to Moshe's concern:

> And the Lord said to Moshe, "*Now* you will see what I will do to Pharaoh, for with a mighty hand he will send them out, and with a mighty hand he will drive them out of his land" (Shemot 6:1).

Hashem told Moshe not to despair, despite the apparent deterioration of the situation. It almost seems as if this was a necessary prelude to the deliverance that would ensue. Of course, the question arises, why is this so? Why did things have to "get worse before they could get better?" The suffering of the Jews had reached the point where the screams brought on by their labors had "gained the attention" of Hashem. Yet the initial consequence of Moshe's intervention was a harshening of their conditions. Why did this have to be?

We cannot fully know or understand the ways of God. We are, however, permitted and encouraged to search for sensible explanations. My own opinion is that Hashem was teaching us important lessons. First, it was necessary to demonstrate Pharaoh's absolutely cruel and obstinate character. Notice that the Jewish foremen had appealed to Pharaoh's sense of justice when they protested the edict of the straw. Apparently, they believed he had some reasonable motives for the enslavement.

Perhaps we can gain some insight into this by studying the behavior of the foremen who were whipped when the Jews failed to meet their quota. They requested a meeting with Pharaoh and poured out their grievances to him. They complained about the injustice of the situation, saying, "why do you treat your servants this way? Straw is not given to your servants, and yet we are commanded to make bricks. Now, your servants are beaten and your people are sinning." (Shemot: 5, 15-16)

Pharaoh responded:

> You are lazy, therefore, you say let us go and sacrifice to the Lord. Now go back to work. Straw shall not be given to you but you must provide the total of bricks." (Shemot 5, 17-18)

We cannot help but be struck by the gap between the pleas of the foremen and the callous response of Pharaoh. How naïve the foremen appear! They were not stupid people but apparently believed that Pharaoh had some basic decency and sense of justice and would agree that the new plan was unfair.

On some level the Jews were able to come to grips with the Egyptian enslavement and did not view their tormentors as absolutely evil. Had things improved immediately upon Moshe's intervention, they would not have attributed it to Hashem, but to the basic decency of the Egyptians. Jews have a tendency to be gullible and believe in the fundamental goodness of all people.

The Jews were not ready for redemption until they shed all illusions about the "fairness" of Egyptian society and acknowledged sheer evil for what it was. Only when they recognized the futility of man-made morality could they appreciate the sublime value of Torah and its *exclusive* capacity to redeem the world.

The Jews did not then know the passage in the Haggadah that states, "If the Holy One, Blessed is He, had not redeemed our forefathers from Egypt, then we and our children and children's children would still be slaves unto Pharaoh in Egypt." The Jews needed to divest themselves of their illusions about the fairness and reasonableness of the regime under which they labored.

In providing straw to his slaves, Pharaoh sought to show that he was a benign and rational ruler who wanted to give his workers all they needed to be "productive." Denying them the straw demonstrated that the enslavement was of a purely destructive nature. He was more intent on tormenting the Jews than on increasing their output.

The Jews could now entertain no doubts about the cruel and intractable nature of Pharaoh and his regime. They finally realized that they were in a situation in which only the "Mighty Hand" of Hashem could liberate them. This explains why the situation had to get worse before it could get better.

This episode also teaches us an important lesson about the nature of our faith in Hashem: It needs to be rooted in a proper foundation. We must be absolutely convinced of Hashem's goodness. It is His essence to be a "faithful God without injustice; He is righteous and upright" (Devarim 32:4). Our belief in Hashem's goodness and trustworthiness cannot be based on the shifting tide of events. We all have our inner scenarios as to how things ought to work out. We have expectations about the outcome of a challenging situation. When things don't go our way, we get depressed and wonder about the ways of God.

We believe that everything Hashem does is for the good, not because of this or that miracle He may have performed for us, but because His *essence* is to do good. This idea is expressed in the fourth blessing of the Grace after Meals, in which we proclaim that "He is the King Who is good and Who does good to all; For every single day He did good, He does good, and He will do good to us."

When things go south and put us in a tailspin, we must remember these vital words. If we retain our faith when matters go badly and seek to get closer to Him in whatever ways we can, He will never let us down, for His compassion is eternal.

The Ability to Discern

In parshat Va'eira, we read about the encounter between Moshe and Pharaoh. Hashem told Moshe what to do when Pharaoh demanded proof that God had spoken to him: Moshe should throw down his staff and it would turn into a snake. He then proceeded to do this before Pharaoh.

> The Lord spoke to Moshe and Aharon saying: "When Pharaoh speaks to you, saying, 'Provide a sign for yourselves,' you shall say to Aharon, 'Take your staff, [and] cast [it] before Pharaoh; it will become a serpent.'"
>
> [Thereupon,] Moshe and Aharon came to Pharaoh, and they did so, as the Lord had commanded; Aharon cast his staff before Pharaoh and before his servants, and it became a serpent. (Shemot 7: 8-10)

Then something strange and unexpected occurred: Pharaoh summoned his magicians and they did the exact same thing!

> [Then,] Pharaoh too summoned the wise men and the magicians, and the necromancers of Egypt also

did likewise with their secret devices. (Shemot, 7:11)

As might be expected, Pharaoh was unimpressed with what Moshe had done and obstinately refused to obey God. The episode concludes with the words, "And Pharaoh hardened his heart and did not listen to them as God had spoken."

The question arises: What was sinful about Pharaoh's behavior? He certainly had a right to demand proof that God had appeared to Moshe. Moreover, he was correct in trying to determine whether or not the deed was truly miraculous. Thus he summoned his magicians and they were able to achieve the same result. We must ask: Why did God give Moshe a sign that could be duplicated by others? Isn't a miracle by definition a supernatural phenomenon, which is beyond the scope of human power and thus can only be attributed to Divine intervention?

If we study the text carefully we can find the answer. Superficially, Moshe's and the magicians' act of turning a staff into a snake appears to be similar. However, they were qualitatively *different*. The Torah says, "And the Egyptian magicians did this with their secret devices." When a skilled magician performs a trick, he controls the environment: He sets up a stage, keeps the audience at a certain distance and manages all of the "props." It is very impressive but we know it is an illusion based on very skillful sleight of hand.

Moshe's miracle was performed in the open without any secret or hidden devices. A truly honest observer would recognize and acknowledge the difference. The verse also points out that Moshe's staff swallowed those of the magicians. Thus Moshe's act was clearly superior to his opponents. If Pharaoh was genuinely interested in the truth, he would have investigated the matter carefully and recognized the difference between Moshe's genuine miracle and the deceptive magic of the illusionists.

Yet we may ask: Why did God give Moshe a

miracle that could be *somewhat* duplicated? Why not give him a sign that could not be imitated at all? The answer is that Hashem wants us to recognize Him through the use of our minds and the exercise of our free will. He doesn't want us to be emotionally coerced into accepting Him. Great miracles impress the emotions but since they don't engage the mind, their effect soon dissipates. Real change is achieved only through genuine knowledge and understanding.

God wants us to use our minds in searching for Him, discovering Him and serving Him. Pharaoh, in fact, *did* sense the significant difference between the miracles of Moshe and the counterfeit displays of his servants. That is why the verse says that "he hardened his heart and did not listen..." Had he not been stubborn, he would have seen the truth. Judaism is unique in affirming the supreme value of knowledge in the service of our Creator. We must, therefore, strive to cultivate a love and appreciation for the Divine Wisdom contained in our Torah.

This parsha has great relevance to our contemporary lives. In every area of significance (religion, societal morality, rightful ownership of Israel) we are challenged by false philosophies that masquerade as truth and ensnare the unlearned. Like Pharaoh, we must choose between the authentic and the illusory. May we fulfill the ideal of the *Havdalah* prayer: May we have the wisdom to discern between the true and the false, the holy and the profane, Israel and the nations.

Bo

Reclaiming One's Dignity

In parshat Bo, we read about the final stage of the enslavement in Egypt. The Jews were not only liberated from physical servitude, they were spiritually redeemed as well. Thus they had to separate themselves from the primitive paganism of Egypt and attach themselves to the commandments of Hashem. They were given the mitzvah of the Passover sacrifice, which was to be performed on their final night in Egypt, as a prerequisite for their liberation.

In anticipation of the Exodus, Moshe, at the behest of Hashem, instructed the people to request gifts of fine clothing and jewelry from their Egyptian neighbors and friends. Surprisingly, the Egyptians responded very generously and gave their best goods to the Jews:

> And the children of Israel did according to Moshe's order, and they borrowed from the Egyptians silver objects, golden objects, and garments.

> The Lord gave the people favor in the eyes of the Egyptians, and they lent them, and they emptied out Egypt. (Shemot: 12:35-36)

At first glance, it is difficult to comprehend why Hashem commanded the Jews to solicit precious items from the Egyptians. Rashi tells us it was in fulfillment of His promise to Avraham that when the Jews would leave the land of their enslavement they would depart with great wealth. However, the method of obtaining the bounty seems strange.

If the purpose of receiving the Egyptians' wealth was in compensation for the forced labor, then Moshe should have demanded it from Pharaoh, who would be obliged to make reparations from Egypt's national treasury. The idea of having each Jewish man and woman approach their Egyptian friends and ask for valuable objects to "borrow" seems strange.

In my opinion, the purpose of the gifts was not for the sake of financial remuneration for forced labor. The worst aspect of the enslavement was the damage it inflicted on the psyche of the Jews. Verbal abuse is a Biblical transgression and in many ways can be more damaging than physical affliction. People who suffer mistreatment often internalize the attitudes of their oppressors and nurture a feeling of self-hate. The Torah is very concerned about the dignity of man, for only a person who feels good about himself can lead a productive life and have a meaningful relationship with Hashem.

Before departing Egypt, Hashem gave the Jews the very significant mitzvah of the Passover sacrifice, whose purpose was to break their attachment to idolatry and initiate them in the Divine service based on Torah and *mitzvot*. However, to serve God properly, a person's psyche must be strong and healthy.

The enslavement had inflicted great damage on the Jews' sense of dignity and self-respect. A person who lacks self-esteem cannot fulfill his purpose in life. God intervened to alter the Egyptians' attitude toward the Jews from one of disdain to a one of awe for them and their fearless leader, Moshe. The Jews now held special favor and charm in the eyes of the Egyptians. Hashem did a lot to help the Jews regain their self-respect; but there are certain things He insists that man must do for himself, in order to complete the process.

The Jews were required to reclaim their dignity by overcoming their inhibitions and "requesting gifts of silver and gold and clothing" from their Egyptian neighbors, so that they could be properly attired when they had their festival to Hashem in the wilderness. The positive reaction of the Egyptians helped rectify the Jews' feelings of worthlessness, created by many generations of enslavement.

The Torah recognizes the vital role of self-esteem in the life of man. We are therefore commanded to show respect for all people, without discrimination, since every person is created in "the image of God." Indeed, the Torah commands us to "love one's friend as oneself." Parshat Bo teaches us that in order to properly respect others, we must first esteem ourselves.

Speaking Truth To Power

Parshat Bo continues the narrative of the ten plagues and the interaction between Moshe and Pharaoh. It's hard to understand Pharaoh's mentality and his refusal to see what had to be clear to everyone. Moshe had dealt charitably with Pharaoh. He respected Pharaoh's intelligence and tried to teach him about the Creator of the Universe who had commanded that he release the Jews to observe a festival to Hashem in the wilderness.

We should note that Moshe did not demand that Pharaoh terminate the enslavement and grant the Jews their freedom. This would have been too much to ask. All that Moshe requested was that the Jews be given some time to fulfill the obligation of serving their God.

Moshe was very gentle with Pharaoh. He used persuasion and demonstrations of Hashem's power, such as converting his staff into a serpent. As Pharaoh hardened his heart, the demonstrations turned to plagues. However, these too were mild, at first. The purpose of the demonstrations and then the plagues was not to inflict pain but to attract the attention of the Egyptians and cause them to consider the matter carefully, and arrive at the proper conclusions.

The plagues ultimately did not produce the desired change in Pharaoh. At times he seemed to be on the brink of capitulation, but he always found some particular point that he couldn't accept. It is amazing to contemplate the enormous devastation that Pharaoh brought down on his land and people. Such is the power of human stubbornness. There is an important lesson for all of us to learn from the reckless behavior of Pharaoh.

How often do we engage in irrational, self-destructive behavior for no good reason other than that of implacable stubbornness? We cannot give in to our evil inclination but must do battle with our emotions on a regular basis. We should develop the ability to be flexible when necessary, to admit we were wrong, and change positions we have clung to when the evidence is clear that we are wrong.

The final encounter between Moshe and Pharaoh took place during the plague of darkness, which paralyzed the Egyptians for three days. Pharaoh was brought to his knees and implored Moshe to "go and serve the Lord." He was even prepared to yield his previous opposition to taking the children with them. However, Pharaoh had one reservation: the Jews could not take all the animals. Moshe responded that they would, indeed, take *all* their cattle, since they could not know what would be needed until they arrived at the place of worship. However, Moshe added a seemingly strange comment. "You too," he said to Pharaoh, "will send sacrifices and burnt offerings which we shall offer to the Lord."

> Pharaoh summoned Moshe and said, "Go! Worship the Lord, but your flocks and your cattle shall be left.

Your young children may also go with you."

But Moshe said, "You too shall give sacrifices and burnt offerings into our hands, and we will make them for the Lord our God." (Shemot 10, 24-25)

The meaning of Moshe's statement is very puzzling, since Pharaoh did not ask Moshe to offer sacrifices for him when he drove the Jews out of Egypt. Another strange outcome of this dialogue is Pharaoh's angry dismissal of Moshe. Until now Pharaoh had been respectful, even admitting guilt before reverting to his chronic recalcitrance. Yet this time he said, "Go from me and watch yourself. Never see my face again for on the day you see my face, you shall die." Seemingly unperturbed, Moshe responded, "as you say, I will never see your face again." (Shemot 10: 28-29)

The question arises, what caused Pharaoh, who had developed an attitude of great respect for Moshe, to suddenly turn against him with anger and threats? In my opinion, Pharaoh's sudden rage was a direct response to Moshe's remark that "he too would send offerings to God." According to the Torah commentator Avraham Ibn Ezra, Moshe was implying that Pharaoh *ought* to send sacrifices to the true God. This infuriated Pharaoh.

Until now Moshe had only pleaded with the Egyptian ruler for the right of the Jews to worship *their* God. Now, he went a step further and pronounced that Hashem was the Master of the Universe and the sole Being whom *all* people had to acknowledge and worship. Moshe thus expounded the principle of "He is our God, there is no other." Moshe demonstrated that it is the mission of the Jewish people to educate all mankind about the folly of idolatry and the imperative to serve the Creator of the Universe. Moshe's implication that Pharaoh's religion was worthless angered him. However, it is the Jewish people's mission to emulate Moshe's courageous example of "speaking truth to power."

The Point Of No Return

Parshat Bo begins with Hashem's instruction to Moshe to "Come to Pharaoh for I have hardened his heart and the heart of his servants in order to place my signs in his midst." (Shemot 10:1)

We must ask: why did Hashem harden Pharaoh's heart? It would seem that the goal of the plagues was to convince the Egyptians of God's existence and absolute mastery of nature, thereby inspiring them to renounce idolatry and embrace the Creator. This is clearly enunciated in the verse that states, "But I will harden Pharaoh's heart and I will increase my signs and my wonders in the land of Egypt … And *Egypt* shall know that I am Hashem, when I stretch out My hand over Egypt; and I shall take the Children of Israel out from among them" (Exodus 7:3-5). If that is the case, it is difficult to comprehend why Hashem would "harden" Pharaoh's heart, since this would seemingly run counter to the stated objective of the signs.

Free will is one of the most fundamental principles of Judaism. Man is endowed with a Divine soul, which enables him to perceive truth and freely choose his life's path. There are no internal or external forces that predetermine the choices he will make. Because man is the master of his moral destiny, he is subject to reward and punishment. The power of free will is such that man is never defeated by sin but always retains the capacity to correct his flaws and return to the path of righteousness. Thus for Judaism, the ability of the sinner to repent is of paramount importance. Hashem says, "I do not desire the death of the sinner but that he abandon his evil path and live." (Ezekiel 18:32)

The worst transgressor has the option to do *teshuva* (repentance) at any point, even on his death bed. If it is genuine, it will be accepted and earn him a share in the world to come. However, according to the Rambam (Maimonides), there is an exception to this rule. He asserts (Mishneh Torah, Laws of Repentance: Chapter 6) that there is a unique punishment reserved for a particular type of sinner whose evil is so egregious that Hashem removes his capacity to repent in order that he receive his just punishment.

Rambam cites Pharaoh as an example of this phenomenon, saying, "Therefore it says in the Torah, 'And I will harden the heart of Pharaoh,' for he sinned of his own accord initially and did evil to the Jews who dwelled in his land. Justice demanded that repentance be withheld from him so that he would be punished and therefore Hashem hardened his heart."

We can now understand why the removal of Pharaoh's free will was essential to achieving Hashem's purpose in bringing down the plagues on Egypt. God wanted to give the Egyptians proof of His existence and absolute power. This required numerous signs and wonders. Each plague displayed a different aspect of Hashem's supreme might and strengthened the growing belief of the people in His existence. Had Pharaoh relented under the pressure of the blows and released the Jews, it would have terminated the "learning experience" of the plagues, which would have been bad for the Egyptians.

The demise of Pharaoh contains a sobering lesson. Our task in life is to perfect our souls through pursuit of truth and righteous behavior. Our most precious asset is the power to choose between good and evil. Every sin strengthens the forces of instinct and weakens our ability to overcome them. Every good deed empowers the soul and enhances our moral capability. Full confidence in our capacity for goodness is essential to our mission in life as individuals and a People. May we always act in a manner that justifies this optimistic attitude.

Beshalach

Love Is *Not* All You Need

Parshat Beshalach recounts one of the greatest miracles in history: the splitting of the Red Sea. The Egyptian expeditionary force was destroyed and the Jewish people were saved. We can imagine the feeling of exhilaration the Jews must have experienced. A short time before they were gripped with panic, sensing imminent doom; many lost their composure and castigated Moshe for bringing them out of Egypt in order to "die in the wilderness."

> Pharaoh drew near, and the children of Israel lifted up their eyes, and behold! The Egyptians were advancing after them. They were very frightened, and the children of Israel cried out to the Lord.
>
> They said to Moshe, Is it because there are no graves in Egypt that you have taken us to die in the desert? What is this that you have done to us to take us out of Egypt?
>
> Isn't this the thing [about] which we spoke to you in Egypt, saying, Leave us alone, and we will serve the Egyptians, because we would rather serve the Egyptians than die in the desert. (Exodus 14: 10-12)

Moshe exhorted them to remain calm in order to experience the salvation of Hashem, who would do battle for them. Now the great miracle had occurred, "and Israel saw the Egyptians dead on the banks of the sea, and the nation feared the Lord and they believed in Hashem and his servant Moshe." (Shemot: 14:31)

How long does inspiration last? The Torah is brutally honest in depicting the behavior of the Jews. "They went three days and did not find water." Just three days after experiencing the miracle of the Red Sea, the people began complaining to Moshe and Aharon.

> Moshe led Israel away from the Red Sea, and they went out into the desert of Shur; they walked for three days in the desert but did not find water.
>
> They came to Marah, but they could not drink water from Marah because it was bitter; therefore, it was named Marah.
>
> The people complained against Moshe, saying, What shall we drink?
> (Shemot 15: 22-24)

The euphoric feeling of salvation evaporated after only three days of travel. We would have expected greater forbearance and a more respectful attitude toward the leaders who had extricated them from bondage and sustained them in their moment of peril. Yet that was not the case. "They went three days and did not find water." Basic human nature asserted itself and they did not rise above mundane emotions.

What lesson can we draw from this? On the midrashic level, the Rabbis teach that the water represents Torah, meaning that the Jews went three days without study. It was this negligence, the Rabbis assert, that caused the Jews to complain. As a result of this episode Moshe ordained public Torah reading on Shabbat, Monday and Thursday, so that the Jews would not go three days without Torah.

There are timely lessons in this rabbinic interpretation. We are all searching for miracles, and experience profound joy when we are fortunate to merit one. Sometimes we bargain with Hashem, saying, "If you would only do such and such for me, I will become a different person." We may be entirely sincere at the moment, but we should always be on guard against self-deception. Powerful emotional experiences do not, of themselves, effectuate lasting change. The reason lies within our psychological makeup. All feelings, no matter how powerful, are bound to wear off. People who are madly in love are convinced that they will feel this way forever and are amazed to discover how mistaken they were.

Our parsha teaches that love, however robust, is a good beginning but it is *not* enough. True and lasting love and growth in a relationship can only come about through steadfast, ongoing efforts. The same applies to every area of our lives. In order to achieve meaningful spiritual growth we must be committed to a program of study, good deeds and honest introspection. Religious inspiration is a wonderful thing but it must be accompanied by diligent effort if we want to reach our full potential. The Rabbis are teaching us that had the Jews been immersed in Torah study, their entire perspective would have been different and they would have handled the water shortage in a more appropriate manner. Torah infuses a person with wisdom and optimism and adds a unique dimension to his *emunah* in Hashem. May we merit to achieve it.

The Leadership of Moshe Rabbenu

In parshat Beshalach, the Jews were seized by panic when they saw the Egyptian army chasing after them, and they turned against Moshe. Their fear was so great that they chastised him for taking them out of Egypt and even claimed that it would have been better for them "to be slaves in Egypt than to die in the wilderness." We can learn a great deal from the reaction of Moshe Rabbenu to this shameful provocation. He did not get angry; he retained his calmness and composure. With the Jews on the verge of a complete meltdown, Moshe encouraged them to stand firm and witness the salvation that Hashem would bring them. Moshe concluded his brief oration with a simple but effective admonition: "Hashem will battle for you and you be silent."

Moshe's behavior in this crisis reflects the qualities of a great leader. In general, even superior, idealistic leaders suffer from a certain vulnerability: the fear of rejection. There is hardly a person who is not affected by harsh criticism. Thus, the science of gauging public opinion has become indispensable to contemporary politicians. Political campaigns are planned with great care and positions taken by candidates are thoroughly tested for public reaction before they are adopted. Even courageous and independent-minded leaders can lose their "cool" when they are accused of bringing great harm upon their people.

Golda Meir, the late Prime Minister of Israel, felt terrible about her responsibility for the catastrophic consequences of allowing Egypt to get in the first blow in the Yom Kippur War. Her grief was so intense that she even considered suicide, but, to her great credit, recognized the impact it would have on the soldiers' morale and decided against it. Menachem Begin spent the last years of his life in a state of withdrawal and depression. There were many causes but clearly the unpopularity of the War in Lebanon and the universal condemnation for the Sabra and Shaltila massacre (which was carried out by Arabs against Arabs and was blamed on Israel) played a significant role.

Moshe Rabbenu was the greatest leader in history. No one ever accomplished more for his people than Moshe, who led the Jews out of Egypt, brought them the Torah and forged them into a nation. Yet Moshe was viciously provoked and personally attacked to the point where he said "just a bit more and they will kill me." Moshe recognized the dangers and pitfalls of leadership and had pleaded with Hashem to be spared that responsibility. His greatest qualification was his lack of ego, which is precisely what attracts ordinary people to positions of power. Often, the very desire for power is rooted in the need of the human ego to be nurtured by the approval of others.

As parents, teachers and spiritual guides, we all are leaders in some sense of the term. Moshe Rabbenu was successful because he was not in search of human recognition. He was absolutely committed to doing what was best for the nation, as dictated by Hashem.   His faith in Hashem was absolute and this alone gave him the strength to act despite the disparagement of mortals.   May we seek to emulate the example of Moshe.   May the Jewish people merit to have spiritual and political leaders who eschew public acclaim and bravely battle for the genuine interests of *Klal Yisrael,* whether popular or not.

Moral Insanity

Parshat Beshalach describes the triumphant Exodus of the Jews from Egypt. The final plague, *makkat bechorot* (slaying of the first born) brought a night of terror upon the entire Egyptian nation. No one was immune. The plague affected everyone, from prisoners in the jails to royalty in the palace. It was a night of horror and mass hysteria. Pharaoh could not withstand the "shock and awe" and sent word to Moshe to depart with his nation immediately and on *his own* terms.

This new state of affairs, in which Pharaoh willingly gave Moshe permission to leave Egypt on his own terms, did not last long. We would think that it would take some time for Pharaoh and his servants to recuperate from the devastation and to return to "normal." It would have made sense for them to lay low, soothe the wounds of the smitten, and seek to learn the lessons of their Divine punishment. Yet none of this occurred. Instead,

Pharaoh's only preoccupation was with bringing the runaway slaves back to Egypt.

We might have thought that Pharaoh would be thrilled to be done with the Jews and have no appetite to tangle with them any further. Yet, amazingly, this was not the case. He regretted that he had released the Jews and organized his entire army to chase them down and capture them. God cooperated with Pharaoh in his plans. He instructed Moshe to lead the Jews in a roundabout path to create the impression that they were lost and disoriented in the wilderness. This was intended to fortify Pharaoh and encourage him to chase after the Jews.

We cannot help but wonder: What motivated Pharaoh to embark on this suicidal mission? Why couldn't he leave well enough alone? Didn't he realize that God was with the Jews and that nothing but harm would result to those seeking to harm them? It's clear that Hashem wanted the confrontation between Pharaoh and the Jews to take place. What motivated Pharaoh to embark on his insane venture and why did Hashem encourage him in this futile endeavor?

We can learn a lot from Pharaoh's irrational behavior. This tyrant and his ilk have appeared many times throughout history. His philosophy, like that of Haman and Hitler, among others, was that "might makes right" and power is the decisive factor in human history. He detested the Jews who repudiated the myth of human strength and proclaimed that God, alone, rules the world.

Moshe insisted that man must conform to Hashem's moral order or face the consequences. When Moshe first conveyed God's command that he allow the Jews to serve Him in the wilderness, Pharaoh retorted, "Who is Hashem that I should listen to His voice? I do not know Hashem and also, I will not send out the Jews."(Exodus 5:2) The purpose of the plagues was to disabuse Pharaoh of his false notions. He needed to know that man has no true power and even the water he drinks can be instantaneously changed into blood. God is all powerful, but He rules the world with justice and compassion. Man must relinquish his arrogance and seek to emulate Hashem who is "Righteous in all His ways."

Pharaoh's pursuit of the Jews into the wilderness illustrates the course of the wicked man. He marches to his own destruction and brings all his subjects down with him. He loses the ability to acknowledge any truth that conflicts with his egotistical illusions. Hashem encouraged Pharaoh to believe that the Jews were lost and vulnerable to attack.

> It was reported to Pharaoh that the people had fled; and Pharaoh and his servants had a change of heart toward the people, and they said, What is this that we have done, that we have released Israel from serving us?

> So he [Pharaoh] harnessed his chariot, and took his people with him.
> (Shemot 14:5-6)

The Rabbis say, "In the direction that a person desires to go, *there* we lead him" (Talmud, Makkot 10b). God does not hinder a person from following his foolish fantasies even as he runs to his own destruction. He has given us free will and endowed us with the ability to think. We are instructed to put our ego aside and choose the good "for our benefit, always." Let us learn the lesson of the tragedy of Pharaoh. Free will and the ability to choose the good is the most precious gift we have. Let us cherish it and use it correctly for, as we know, improper choices can produce devastating effects. They can lead to a situation in which we can no longer see the difference between good and evil. The story of Pharaoh's mad journey to destruction illustrates that when he embraced the evil path, God did not deter him from the consequences of his moral insanity.

In the Blink of an Eye

Parshat Beshalach describes the hasty departure of the Jews from Egypt. The Rabbis say "the salvation of Hashem is like the blink of an eye." (Pesikta Zutreta, Esther 4:17) In other words, it comes suddenly and quickly and not as a natural result of a lengthy process. Thus, a defining feature of *geula* (redemption) is that it is instantaneous. One minute the Jews were abject slaves completely under the totalitarian domination of Pharaoh. With the advent of *makkat bechorot* (slaying of Egyptian first born) the situation changed immediately, and the slave masters couldn't push the Jews out of the land quickly enough. Indeed, the Egyptians actually wanted the Jews to leave that very night. However, Moshe refused: he was now in control and could set the terms by which his people would depart.

According to the Rabbis, the spiritual redemption of the Jews took place by night, when they brought the Passover sacrifice and witnessed the complete collapse of the Egyptian political apparatus. Moshe did not want the Jews to slink out of Egypt like "thieves in the night." Instead, they would leave by day in an organized fashion, the triumphant "Hosts of Hashem," in the sight of all.

Rabbi Joseph B. Soloveitchik ("the Rav") explained that the significance of matzah is related to the haste of the redemption. Anything that is part of the natural order requires time. The leavening process needs time. For that reason, leavened bread is prohibited on Passover, since it symbolizes the natural order. Matzah, however, is baked immediately before the dough has had time to rise, thus representing the Divine providence which overpowers the natural order. We eat matzah and avoid *chametz* (leaven) to proclaim that the freedom we achieved with the Exodus was not due to any natural historical development, but only to the miraculous intervention of the Creator of the Universe. Rabbi Soloveitchik states:

> In my opinion, Rabban Gamliel wanted to say that genuine *ge'ulah*, genuine redemption, always comes

suddenly, unexpectedly, at a time when people are ready to give up hope. Sometimes historical situations continue to deteriorate; people pray and cry, begging for mercy—but there is no answer to prayer, only silence. At that moment, when the crisis reaches its maximum and threatens the very existence of the community, when people begin to give up, the ge'ulah suddenly comes and takes them out of the land of affliction. It comes in the middle of the night and knocks on the door when no one expects it, when everybody is skeptical about it, when everybody laughs off the possibility of redemption. (Festival of Freedom: Essays on Pesah and the Hagaddah, 84-85)

Saw You at Sinai

In describing the Exodus from Egypt, the Torah mentions that Moshe took the bones of Yosef with him, for Joseph had made the children of Israel swear, saying 'Hashem will certainly remember you and you shall take my bones with you.' (Exodus 13:19) The question arises: Why does the Torah include this piece of information as a central part of the narrative of the Exodus? Of course it is important for the Torah to emphasize the significance of fulfilling an oath. But Yosef's oath was very unique. He did not obligate any particular person; rather, he obligated the entire Jewish people. When Yosef's brothers accepted the responsibility of taking Yosef's bones out of Egypt, they did so on behalf of the Jewish Nation including future unborn generations.

Between the time of Yosef's death and the Exodus, every generation of Jews confirmed and accepted the obligation of this oath. This oath thus assumed the status of a national responsibility and it was the obligation of the leader to fulfill it. On that hectic night, with so much to do, Moshe put everything aside and personally saw to the securing of Yosef's bones. Why is this action so central to the redemption from Egypt?

In my opinion it was not just a matter of fulfilling a national responsibility, however significant. Hashem had told Moshe that when he took the Jews out of Egypt, "they would serve Him on this Mountain." In other words, the reason Hashem was taking them out of Egypt was because the Jews would accept the Torah on Mt. Sinai. However, the Jews of that time did not just accept the Torah for themselves, but for all future generations. This, in my opinion, is the meaning of the Rabbinic dictum that the souls of all Jews who would ever be born were present at Sinai. Every Jew is obligated to keep the Torah because he swore to it at Sinai. The ability of the Jews at Sinai to assume a national responsibility that is binding on all future generations is at the heart of why Hashem chose them to be His people and perpetuate His Torah.

That is why it was so important for Moshe to personally assume the responsibility of transporting the bones of Yosef on the journey to Canaan. It reminded everyone that Yosef was the instrument of Divine Providence in bringing the Jews down to Egypt. Their enslavement and ultimate redemption was all part of Hashem's plan to create a special nation that would be "a light unto the nations" and the means by which mankind would eventually be redeemed. That could only happen if every generation of Jews would view themselves as bound by the oath taken at Sinai. Moshe set the example by assuming responsibility for the oath taken by Yosef's brothers and passed down by every generation until the Exodus. May we always regard ourselves as sworn to keep the Torah from Sinai.

Yisro

Have You Heard?

Parshat Yisro begins by telling us that Yisro, Moshe's father-in-law, *heard* the news of the great events surrounding the Exodus of the Jews from Egypt. At first glance, the statement "and Yisro heard" seems completely unnecessary. Of course he heard! Who didn't hear? The Exodus and destruction of the Egyptian army at the Red Sea were events of international magnitude that became known throughout the world. Moshe attests to the far-reaching impact of the great miracle in the *Shirat Hayam* ("Song at the Sea")

> People heard, they trembled; a shudder seized the inhabitants of Philistia. Then the chieftains of Edom were startled; [as for] the powerful men of Moab, trembling seized them; all the inhabitants of Canaan melted. May dread and fright fall upon them; with the arm of Your greatness may they become as still as a stone, until Your people cross over, O Lord, until this nation that You have acquired crosses over. (Shemot: 15: 14-16)

Indeed, these events created such a powerful impression that 40 years later, Rachav told the spies sent by Joshua into Israel:

> I know that the Lord has given you the land, and that your terror is fallen upon us, and that all the inhabitants of the land have melted away because of you.

> For we have heard how the Lord dried up the water of the Red Sea for you when you came out of Egypt; and what you did to the two kings of the Amorites that were on the other side of the Jordan, Sihon and Og, whom you completely destroyed. (Joshua 2: 9-10)

It is clear that the Exodus was a very well-known event. We must also assume that Yisro, whose own son-in-law was at the center of it, carefully followed what was unfolding. Why, then, would the Torah waste words by saying, "And Yisro heard?"

The Hebrew term "*Shema*" (hear) denotes more than simple listening. It connotes comprehension of the significance of what is being said. When we recite the "*Shema*," "Hear O Israel Hashem Our God is One," we mean that one should contemplate the meaning and importance of this idea, which is the foundation of the Jewish religion. Thus, "*Vayishma Yisro*" (and Yisro heard) is not telling us that he heard the news of the Exodus, but rather that he comprehended its deeper meaning and recognized that there was very much he needed to learn about it.

Yisro's "hearing" was different from everyone else's. It was unique and special. Others heard the news superficially. They were momentarily excited but that feeling wore off. For Yisro, the events were an intellectual game-changer. Why? Because he was the rarest of people: a genuine thinker who was searching for religious truth. He was not content with ordinary, mindless faith. Rashi (Exodus: 18:11) states that Yisro investigated all the religious cults of the time and discarded each one after discovering their emptiness.

This passion for knowledge and understanding was the reason Yisro journeyed to meet Moshe at his wilderness encampment. After their reunion, the two spent much time together as Moshe conveyed the deeper meaning of all that God had done for His people in Egypt and in the desert after the Exodus. Yisro sought a more profound understanding of the spiritual implications of these awesome events. As a result of his learning sessions with Moshe, Yisro was transformed into a new person. He became both the father-in-law and disciple of this great man. He converted to Judaism, made a great contribution to the Jewish people, and merited to have the parsha that contains the *Aseret Hadibrot* (Ten "Commandments") named after him. Now we can understand why the Torah saw fit to point out that "Yisro heard."

Yisro's Blessing

After Yisro fully understood Moshe's in-depth account of the Exodus from Egypt, the Torah states:

> Yisro said, "Blessed is the Lord, Who has rescued you from the hands of the Egyptians and from the hand of Pharaoh, Who has rescued the people from beneath the hand of the Egyptians." (Exodus 17:10)

The Rabbis note that although the Jews had sung praises to God after the splitting of the Red Sea, no one *blessed* Him for the miracle of the Exodus, until Yisro. He was the first to bless Hashem for the Exodus because for him, the Exodus was a transformative experience in terms of his relationship with God. He was the kind of person King David refers to when he said, "My soul thirsts for the Lord, the living God" (Tehillim 42:2), which I take to refer to the true God and not the imaginary deity of superficially religious people.

Yisro's honest search for true closeness with God, and his success at achieving it, illustrates the Rabbis' teaching that when "one comes to purify himself he receives assistance" (Talmud Shabbat

104). When a person seeks out Hashem in earnest, he will never be disappointed. Yisro renounced idolatry and searched for the true God. Hashem sent him Moshe and he made the most of that opportunity. After hearing Moshe's explication of all that had occurred during the Exodus, Yisro declared:

> Now I know that the Lord is greater than all the deities, for with the thing that they (the Egyptians) plotted, [He came] upon them. (Exodus 18:11)

Indeed, part of what led Yisro to "bless" Hashem, and grow close to Him, was that he truly "heard" what Moshe had to say. We too can learn about drawing close to Hashem through Yisro. As it says in the opening words of our parsha, "And Yisro heard." Hashem had revealed Himself to the entire world through the great miracles. He performed these wonders for Israel. Yet how many people truly *heard* the message of the miracles? How many were motivated to open their minds, inquire, gain new understanding and elevate themselves to a higher spiritual plane? How many took advantage of the opportunity that was knocking at their door?

All the miracles in the world are of no lasting importance unless they stimulate us to become actively involved in the pursuit of wisdom and spiritual growth. Although God may favor some of us with miraculous experiences, unless these events are accompanied by dedicated efforts of study and honest inquiry, they will not have enduring impact.

Even the Jews who experienced the wonders of the Exodus and the giving of the Torah at Mount Sinai were not immune from doubts and sin. Only three days after being saved from the Egyptian army through the splitting of the Red Sea, the Jewish people complained to Moshe about being brought out of Egypt to die of thirst in the desert! We see clearly that God's miraculous intervention *alone* is not enough if we don't also do our part through diligent study and personal effort. As it is written in the Ethics of the Fathers: "If I am not for myself, who will be for me?" (Ethics of the Fathers, 1:14).

May the story of Yisro's burning thirst for knowledge, his willingness to listen and learn, be a source of inspiration to us, God's chosen people.

Faith: Is it Contrary to Reason?

Parshat Yisro describes the greatest event in history: the Revelation of God at Mount Sinai and His proclamation of the *Aseret Hadiberot* (Ten Commandments) before a gathering of the entire nation. What was the purpose of this event? Clearly it was the will of Hashem to communicate His Torah to His chosen people. This revelation, however, was accomplished through Moshe.

Moshe was the most unique person in history, a special creation of Hashem who reached a level of prophecy in which he communicated "face to face," at will, with God. The Torah itself testifies that there never was, nor ever will be, another prophet like Moshe, with regard to the level of Divine knowledge he attained and the magnitude of the miracles he performed. (Devarim 34:10)

God chose Moshe to be His emissary to the Jews and to Pharaoh. Moshe, in his great humility, initially refused the assignment on the grounds that he was unqualified for such an exalted mission. He pleaded with Hashem to relieve him of this task and to confer it on someone more qualified. From this we learn what makes not just a great leader, but a great person. Like Moshe, we need to cultivate the virtue of humility, which the Rambam says is the quality most essential to human perfection. Striving for humility does not mean we should foster a false sense of inadequacy; indeed, we should develop our skills and constantly seek to improve ourselves. However, we should also have a realistic sense of our limitations and refrain from pushing ourselves into positions we are not qualified for.

True humility enables us to acknowledge our flaws and seek to correct them. It relieves us of the need to maintain a public image that is not in line with reality. A truly humble person is at peace with himself, not envious of others, and appreciates all the blessings in his life without feeling disappointed that he doesn't get what he feels he deserves. Moshe Rabbenu was truly humble as he did not desire any of the honor associated with positions of authority. Hashem, however, insisted that he was the one to lead the Jews out of Egypt. Moshe was left with no choice but to reluctantly accept. It appears that Moshe's concerns about his inadequacies were not borne out:

> So the Lord gave the people favor in the Egyptians' eyes; also the man Moshe was highly esteemed in the eyes of Pharaoh's servants and in the eyes of the people. (Shemot 11:3)

There are those who say that the "people" referred to here are the Jews. They accepted Moshe as their leader and as a genuine prophet who communicated the word of God. Thus they fulfilled the commands to offer the Passover sacrifice in Egypt and to request gifts of the Egyptians. They followed Moshe into the wilderness and obeyed the instructions he issued. After the destruction of the Egyptian army in the Red Sea the verse states, "and they believed in Hashem and in His servant Moshe."

> And the people *believed*, and they heard that the Lord had remembered the children of Israel, and they

kneeled and prostrated themselves. (Exodus 4:31)

Why, then, was it necessary for Hashem to make an appearance before the entire nation? Why could He not continue with the plan of communicating His will through Moshe?

The Jewish notion of faith is different than that of any other religion. Religious people are proud of the fact that they have faith in God even though they cannot claim knowledge of His existence. They think it is a virtue to "believe" even though they have no certitude. Judaism is different. It does not extol blind faith; instead, it exhorts man to strive for the highest possible level of knowledge. True faith emerges from the rational part of man, who attains a conviction of the existence of God through contemplation of His great works, which display His infinite wisdom. Moshe prayed to Hashem:

> And now, if I have indeed found favor in Your eyes, pray let me know Your ways, so that I may *know* You, so that I may find favor in Your eyes; and consider that this nation is Your people. (Shemot 33:13)

God finds favor with those who strive to know Him and in the words of the Rambam, our love of God is proportional to our knowledge; the more we know Him, the more we love Him. In our religion, ignorance is an *obstacle* to our wholehearted service of Hashem. That is why Hashem was not content to reveal Himself only through the agency of Moshe. True, Moshe performed the most wondrous and impressive miracles. However, the Rambam says, one who believes because of miracles always retains some doubt and suspicion. Miracles are not entirely satisfying to man's intellect. Hashem wanted to eliminate all doubt and make His Existence and Will known in a manner that would satisfy the minds of the Jews. He convened the entire people, allowing them to witness supernatural phenomena and hear a voice from Heaven speaking directly to them, proclaiming the Ten Commandments. Thus, when Moshe exhorted the Jews to observe the Torah, he did not call on them to have faith. Rather he said to them:

> You have been shown, in order to *know* that the Lord He is God; there is none else besides Him. (Devarim14:35)

An entire nation witnessed with its own eyes the existence of God and the proclamation of His Torah. No other religion would dare to make such a claim. All other religions are based on blind faith, without a shred of evidence to substantiate their assertions. Only Judaism elevates the mind of man and extols knowledge as the most significant factor in the *authentic* service of Hashem. This is why the very first request we make in our weekday prayers is for wisdom and discernment. May we merit to achieve them and constantly grow in our knowledge and love of Hashem.

Mishpatim

The True Test of Piety

Parshat *Mishpatim*, deals with civil laws that govern the interactions of people, especially those having economic consequences. Theft, property damage and physical assault are some of the topics touched upon in this portion of the Torah. While there is no doubt about the practical necessity for these ordinances, we need to understand their religious significance. Ramban (Nachmanides) quotes the *Midrash* which states, "The entire Torah depends on justice; therefore the Holy One gave the civil laws after the *Aseret Hadibrot*" (the Ten Commandments).

At first glance this statement is puzzling. Religion is generally associated with "spiritual" activities such as prayer, study and *mitzvot*. While everyone acknowledges the need for appropriate social behavior, its religious importance is not readily apparent. To grasp the Torah's outlook on this matter, we can note a disparity in the way some observant people relate to rituals as opposed to ethics. Some may pray with great fervor and be exceedingly strict in what they accept as kosher, yet fail to display the same intense meticulousness in their treatment of others and conduct of business.

Our parsha is teaching us the supreme religious importance of ethical and moral behavior, especially as it relates to others. All of the laws of Mishpatim can be subsumed under the banner of "You shall love your fellow as yourself." This ideal has been challenged as unrealistic since it is contrary to the selfish nature of man.

Let us admit that we are narcissistic beings whose primary concern is for our personal gratification. Is it reasonable to demand that we love every Jew as we love ourselves? There are, of course, certain relationships in which one values his "fellow" so much that he will relinquish everything, if need be, for his welfare. Parents are prepared to sacrifice their lives for the sake of their children. However, the Torah goes far beyond these limited instances and requires that we love *every* Jew, even a total stranger, as we love ourselves. How is this possible to achieve?

Hillel the great Talmudic sage, provided a brilliant exposition of this imperative. He said, "That which is distasteful to you, do not do unto others." We are obliged to treat others as we would want them to treat us. The Rambam teaches that just as we are concerned for our welfare, property and honor, so should we be solicitous of the dignity and sensitivities of others. This is contrary to our natural inclinations. We are very resentful of the slightest insult, real or imagined, yet are generally not as concerned with the feelings of others.

The Torah teaches that we cannot determine our behavior toward fellow humans on the basis of our emotions. This is a true test of our connection to Hashem. If our love of God is of the narrow, self serving kind, in which we serve Him for the sake of what He will do for us, then our primary attraction will be to the ritualistic aspects of Judaism. We will pray with great focus and perform *mitzvot* conscientiously because this caters to our desire for Divine protection. A person with this orientation will not be as attracted to those commandments in which we are bidden to do things for the benefit of others, especially if they are *strangers*.

We are exhorted by the parsha of Mishpatim to strive for the level of one who serves Hashem out of love and not only for personal reward. Such a person cultivates a sense of awe for all of God's creations which are reflections of His infinite wisdom and compassion. This affects his attitude toward *all* his fellow human beings. He does not regard himself as the center of the universe. Rather, he considers himself to be a special creation of Hashem whose uniqueness lies in the "Divine" soul with which he has been endowed.

His respect for others is based on his awareness that they *too* have been "created in God's image" and as such are entitled to the same rights and privileges he enjoys by the will of Hashem. He realizes that all people are equal in the sight of their Creator, and that mistreatment of others violates the will of Hashem and negates the fundamental principle of "In the Image of God He created him, male and female created He them." (Genesis: 1:27).

We can now understand why the entire Torah is contingent on justice. The purpose of all the *mitzvot* is to perfect our nature through recognition and love of Hashem. No area of Torah requires that we overcome our primal narcissism and act in accordance with objective truth more than that of ethical and just behavior in our dealings with others. The meticulous fulfillment of these laws can elevate us to the level of those who serve Hashem out of love. That is the objective of the entire Torah. May we merit to attain it.

Finders Keepers?

The main theme of parshat Mishpatim is the civil laws that govern inter-personal relations and thus assure the smooth functioning of an orderly society. Thus, many of the Torah laws regarding liability for damages and criminal actions are spelled out in great detail. In addition to these regulations, the *parsha* obligates us in unique acts of kindness to our fellow Jews. For example, we are required to assume responsibility and see to the return of the lost objects of our brethren.

We should appreciate the full significance of this *mitzvah*. In our secular society one is not legally bound to return lost objects. As the popular saying goes, "finders keepers losers weepers." Whenever a person goes out of his way and does return a wallet or other object of value he is regarded as someone very special. However, a Jew has no option in this matter. It is a *mitzvah* of the Torah to care for and return lost objects.

It is interesting to pay attention to the language that the Torah employs in formulating this commandment. The verse states: "If you encounter an ox of your enemy or his donkey wandering, you shall return it." (Shemot: 23:4) As we know from the Talmud, this verse is referring to the lost object of *any* fellow Jew. Usually when specifying obligations we have to other Jews, the Torah utilizes the words "friend" or "brother." For example: "You shall love your friend as yourself" (Vayikra: 9:17) or "You shall not hate your brother in your heart." (Vayikra 19:17).

The Torah employs these terms to teach us that all Jews are part of *one family* and should regard and treat each other with the concern we would extend to our loved ones. Why then, in the matter of returning lost objects, does the Torah make reference to the property of one's *enemy*? Ideally, of course, all of Israel would be one happy family with great mutual respect and affection. Unfortunately, however, we are not quite there yet.

We are a much divided people and have not, as of now, elevated ourselves above the sin of baseless hatred. So while we have many friends we sometimes have enemies, or people we dislike intensely. Perhaps they have offended or mistreated us for no good reason and, to put it bluntly, we just "can't stand them." What happens if you notice an object on the street and instantly recognize that it belongs to this "lowlife" who has been treating you in an abusive manner? Your immediate instinct is to simply move on. Why should I have to bother with *his* lost property? Too bad! He deserves it!

The Torah, however, maintains that this is a genuine test of one's character. The truly godly person does not act according to the dictates of his emotions. He doesn't only serve Hashem when it feels pleasant and is in line with his innate sense of right and wrong. He is humble and submits to the will of Hashem who is the ultimate arbiter of what is good and what is evil.

The Torah is teaching that we must overcome our natural inclination and act in accordance with the instructions of Hashem, even when it is painful to the ego. The one who returns the lost object of his "friend" is performing a very significant *mitzvah*. The one who returns the property of his enemy is operating on the highest level of perfection.

Measure for Measure

The Torah has many rules regarding one's responsibilities towards others. It is especially demanding with regard to the manner in which we must treat someone's property. We must do our utmost to avoid causing monetary damage to our fellow man. It goes without saying that we must be even more careful not to inflict bodily harm on anyone. The Torah spells out the punishment for physical violence in stark detail.

> But if other damage ensues, the penalty shall be life for life, eye for eye, tooth for tooth, hand for hand, foot for foot, burn for burn, wound for wound, and bruise for bruise. (Exodus 21:23-25)

Few verses of the Torah have caused as much misunderstanding as this one. Many self-styled "theologians" have castigated Judaism as being a religion of revenge and not mercy. They failed to consider other statements in this *parsha* which warn us to not stand idly by the blood of our brother, return the lost objects of even a complete stranger, and to come to the assistance of one's "enemy" whose animal has fallen under its load. The Torah teaches us that God's mercies extend to all His creatures and we are enjoined from causing pain even to animals.

The truth is that no people are as compassionate as the Jews. Israeli medical treatment, the most advanced in the Middle East, is dispensed equally to Jew and Arab alike. When Palestinians, regardless of their politics, have serious medical issues, they choose an Israeli hospital over an Arab one, every time. Israel provides treatment to Syrians wounded by their own government in spite of the fact they get no credit for it. When disaster strikes anywhere, the Israelis, with their advanced field hospitals and cutting-edge techniques, are the first to arrive and save lives.

The Jewish people are accurately described in the Talmud as "merciful ones, who are children of merciful ones." Those who malign the Jews are guilty of evil speech and defamation of character. It is *they* who harbor cruelty which they project onto Israel. What then is the meaning of the verses which call for the punishment of "an eye for an eye?"

All of the laws of the Torah are defined and elucidated by the Oral explanations which Hashem gave to Moshe on Sinai and which have been transmitted to the leading Torah scholars of every generation up to the present day. The Talmud makes clear that these verses are not to be taken literally, but rather are referring to monetary compensation. According to the Talmud, there was never a court in Jewish history that extracted an "eye for an eye." Rather, the intention was to pay the monetary worth of the limb, which the offender destroyed.

Proof that this is the case is the fact that there are many chapters in the Talmud dealing with the complicated legal matter of assessing the monetary value of human limbs and organs. Not to mention the evaluation of collateral damages such as pain, unemployment, embarrassment, etc. The notion that Jewish jurisprudence took the injunction of a limb for limb literally is ignorant at best and malicious at worst.

One may ask, if the true intention of the Torah is to exact monetary indemnities for bodily harm, why doesn't it say so outright? Why use language which clearly implies that the exact physical damage inflicted by the perpetrator of the assault will be visited on him?

The great sage Rabbi Joseph B. Soloveitchik provided a fascinating explanation. The Torah, he said, is concerned with justice. Absolute justice is based on the principle of "measure for measure." One who has the cruelty to remove the limb of his friend has lost the ability to empathize with the suffering of the "other." True justice demands that he be made to experience the same pain he inflicted, in order to know what it feels like and repent for his ruthlessness.

On the highest level of justice, man needs to suffer an "eye for an eye." However, the Creator, in His mercy, recognized the inability of people to sustain such punishment and allowed for a substitute of monetary compensation. When making the payment, the offender should pause and remember that he truly deserves to lose his limb, but the restitution is an expression of Divine mercy which, hopefully, he will now display towards all of God's creatures. To label Judaism as a religion of revenge is foolish and malicious slander. To the contrary, it is the religion of true compassion, i.e., that which integrates the highest level of justice and mercy.

The Path of Return

The commandments of the Torah are divided into two groups known as "between man and God" and "between man and man." Prohibitions about forbidden foods, sexual relations, etc. are examples of the first category. The injunction against slander and the obligation to return lost objects are examples of directives pertaining to our responsibilities to others. The question arises, which of the two categories of *mitzvot* presents the greater challenge?

It should be noted that there are differences in the consequences that result from violations of the laws between man and God as opposed to those between man and man. No one is perfect and human beings by nature are prone to sin. This is, by no means, the doctrine that man is *evil by nature* which certain forms of Christianity espouse. Judaism is the only religion, in my opinion, which is founded on the principle of the perfectibility of human nature. Man is not in need of any extraneous mechanism of salvation. His destiny is completely in his own hands. He is a sinner by nature because he starts out in an imperfect state, and his task is to correct his defects and do what is good.

Hashem knew that we are bound to sin at times and in His mercy gave us the opportunity of *teshuva* (repentance). The power of *teshuva* is so great that it can secure atonement for even the most egregious sins. According to the Rambam no sin is beyond the redemptive effects of *teshuva*. Even if a person has been a sinner all of his life and does genuine *teshuva* at the very end, he is forgiven and has a share in the world to come. This is an example of supreme magnanimity in the authentic religion of mercy and compassion.

I would, however, caution against an attitude of complacency in confronting one's sins. One should not feel that there is *no rush* and, worst case, he can always repent "later." No one knows what the future has in store for him, and if he puts it off he may never get the chance to renounce his sins. Even if he does have the opportunity, it is unlikely that one who is entrenched in a sinful way of life will see the light when his time is up. The wise person should not put off the most important decision pertaining to his existence in this world and the one to come. The return to Hashem is an urgent necessity which should never be postponed.

The awareness that Hashem is benevolent and always desires our *teshuva* should be a permanent part of our consciousness. Even when committing a serious sin one should not despair for he can rectify the lapse and be forgiven. However, he must realize that not all sins are the same, in terms of *teshuva*. Sin between man and God is much simpler to atone. In such a case one must come before his Creator, with sincere contrition and resolve to abandon the transgression he has committed.

However, sins between man and man are more difficult to repair. Before confessing to God one must make amends with the aggrieved party and solicit his forgiveness. This is a much more challenging task. One can conquer his pride and humbly admit wrongdoing before the Creator of the universe.

It is not so easy to put ego aside and admit you were wrong to a person you offended. Even if you muster the strength to do this, you must still face the possibility that your apology won't be accepted and you will have a very tough time obtaining forgiveness. *Hashem* is all merciful but humans can be a mean, unforgiving lot. There are people who simply can never let go of a slight and will not let you off the hook.

When we deal harshly or insensitively with others we are often not even aware that we have hurt them. Or, it's possible that we did harm to a group of people and will not have the chance to track each one down and straighten out the mess. Perhaps that is why the first set of laws are the social ordinances. For many people, it is easier to observe the personal restrictions and obligations which are purely between man and Hashem.

In general it is easier to give honor to Hashem, and the laws between man and God are intended for our personal benefit. It is more difficult to overcome pride and be respectful of the dignity and rights of others. Judaism demands that we follow the Torah in the area of personal, ritual requirements and *equally* adhere to the high standards of justice and respect that it requires us to maintain towards others. Let us remember that in respecting people we are giving honor to Hashem who created each person "in His image." In that sense every commandment is, at bottom, between man and God. We honor our Creator by demonstrating love for those creatures that He endowed with a Divine soul.

Terumah

God's "Dwelling Place"

Parshat Terumah deals with the construction of the *Mishkan* (Tabernacle) in the wilderness. Precise details were transmitted regarding the materials that were to be used, dimensions of the structure, as well as the vessels that would be needed. The purpose of the edifice is stated at the outset:

> And they shall make Me a sanctuary and I will dwell in their midst. (Shemot 25:8)

Some questions arise. First of all, what is the meaning of the idea that God "dwells among us?" In addition, the voluntary manner of securing the materials for the *Mishkan* is unusual. Our relationship to the Creator is based on the idea of *mitzvot* (commandments). The Torah is not a book of advice and suggestions. Hashem's will is incorporated into the 613 mitzvot which we are obligated to perform.

Parenthetically, the concept of commandments runs counter to the mentality of modern man, including many "accommodationist" rabbis who are willing to alter Torah obligations that are out of sync with the contemporary mindset.

At this point in time man believes in *himself* and feels that his sense of right and wrong is supreme. He dislikes the notion of an objective truth and an absolute Ruler of the universe to whose authority one must conform. The Torah, however, recognizes the shallowness of this attitude and affirms that man can elevate his nature only by *submission* to the Divine Will. If that is the case, we would have expected the Jews to have been *commanded* to provide the objects needed for the *Mishkan*. Yet, that is not the way it happened. Hashem instructed Moshe to take donations from anyone "whose heart motivated him to give:"

> The Lord spoke to Moshe saying: Speak to the children of Israel, and have them take for Me an offering; from every person whose heart inspires him to generosity, you shall take My offering. (Exodus 25: 1-2)

No one was obligated to contribute, as the giving had to come from the heart. Thus, our second question is why, in contradistinction to *tzedaka* (charity), which we are mandated to give, did God see fit to have the *Mishkan* established on a purely non-compulsory basis?

In addressing our questions, it is important to realize that the very notion of a *Mishkan* is problematic. The most fundamental idea of Judaism is that God is absolutely incorporeal. We cannot attribute to Him any physical qualities. He exists, eternally, outside of time and space. Therefore, in a strict sense, it is idolatrous to maintain that God "resides" in a particular spot. Yet, on a superficial level, our parsha seems to be making the point that Hashem "dwells" in the *Mishkan*. How are we to reconcile this with our doctrine of Divine incorporeality?

To resolve this problem, we must pay careful attention to the exact wording of the verse. It says,

"They shall make a Sanctuary for me and I will dwell among them." Scripture does not state that Hashem resides *in* the Sanctuary, as such a notion would be blasphemous. Rather, the verse contains two ideas: the Jews should make a Sanctuary which is dedicated to Hashem's name, and that if they do, He will "dwell among them." To "dwell among them" means that He will manifest His providential relationship in their midst.

When the people He has chosen adheres to His Torah and reflects its infinite wisdom in every area of individual and communal life, they will be worthy of His protection. When the Jews act in a Godly manner and all their endeavors are crowned with success, people will take notice. This was the case with Yosef, whose success in the house of Potiphar was so great that his master was convinced that *Hashem* was "with him" in all that he did. The national mission of the Jewish People is to sanctify the name of God in the world. When the Jews rise to this level, all mankind will seek to become holy by renouncing idolatry and hedonism and embracing worship of the true God as elucidated in His Torah.

We can now understand why the Jews were not *commanded* to make contributions for the building of the *Mishkan*. Had it been done this way, the people would have viewed the *Mishkan* as another religious obligation. The *Mishkan*, however, is much more than a structure in which the sacrificial service is performed. It is, in addition, a place which serves to remind us of the Creator of the Universe and the moral order which He established for mankind. The great medieval commentator Ramban, explains that the Sanctuary was designed to be an eternal reminder of the Revelation on Mt. Sinai. There, God "spoke" to an entire nation which had gathered to witness the Revelation.

In this encounter the Jewish people reached an exalted level of prophecy. The experience transformed them into a "Kingdom of Priests and a Holy Nation." As a result of this, they attained a profoundly intense love of God that generated a passion to publicize His name in the world. Only *this* spirit and desire could be the motivation for constructing the *Mishkan.* Hashem, therefore, instructed Moshe to take donations, *only* from those whose hearts elevated them to participate.

Many lessons can be derived from Hashem's decree to "take from anyone whose heart inspires him to give". One of the greatest tests of character is the acquisition of extreme financial gain. People fantasize about winning the lottery and are convinced it will transform them to a state of permanent bliss. However, *nothing* is further from the truth. Many lives have been ruined because of extreme wealth. Judaism does not disparage economic success. God bestowed abundant largess on the patriarchs and promised Avraham that his descendants would not leave Egypt "empty handed." In fact, the booty that the Jews retrieved from the drowned Egyptian army at the Red Sea was greater than all they had taken when they "cleaned out

Egypt." Hashem conducted the most massive transfer of funds in history.

According to the great commentator Ibn Ezra, the Jews were not guilty of deceit in "borrowing" valuables from the Egyptians with no intention of returning them. For, he says, the Jews did this at the behest of Hashem who is the owner of all the earth's resources. He gave wealth to the Egyptians and when they sinned He took it from them and gave it to the Jews. However, wealth, per se, is not a blessing as its misuse causes great harm.

Through the building of the *Mishkan*, Hashem imparted a lesson about the proper use of money. It is a blessing when it is associated with true values and is used to secure them. When the call went out for the materials needed for the *Mishkan*, the Jews realized why Hashem had entrusted them with great wealth. It was to enable them to be actively involved in the construction of the *Mishkan*. It is also true that one who is involved in the establishment of a sanctuary will become, thereby, dedicated to its ongoing activities and ideals.

The proper use of wealth is one of the most important teachings of the Torah. One who gives generously to a noble cause experiences great spiritual benefit and joy. He affirms that Hashem is the master of the universe who dispenses material blessings so that righteous people can use them to bring goodness to the world. We should strive to cultivate a discerning heart and a generous spirit, and give of ourselves and our resources with love.

Serve *Only* Hashem

The *Mishkan* was the designated place where Hashem would "manifest His Presence" and providential protection of the Jewish people. The physical structure of the *Mishkan* did not by itself guarantee God's presence. Hashem said "And they shall make *for Me* a Tabernacle and I will dwell among them." (Shemot 25:8) Rashi elucidates this verse:

> And they shall make Me a sanctuary: And they shall make in My name a house of sanctity.

There are two very important ideas contained in this Rashi. The Sanctuary must be consecrated to *His* name, which represents the authentic idea of God that is unique to the Jewish people. We must divest ourselves of any false notions of Hashem, which stem from the idolatrous emotions of man.

A key aspect of our *emunah* (faith) is the affirmation that "He is our God there is no other." We can't put our faith in any other being, even if we believe in Hashem as well. We must worship Him

121

exclusively and not believe that any person, no matter how holy, or object, no matter how sacred, can achieve anything for us in our time of need. We must cultivate a pure *emunah* in which we turn *only* to Hashem for *all* of our needs and desires.

This trust in Hashem also demands that we serve Him *only* in the manner in which He has instructed us. We must adhere to faithful performance of His *mitzvot* and not add to or subtract from them. The ideal of meticulous adherence to the exact commands of Hashem, is expressed in the very construction of the *Mishkan*. The Torah goes into all of the most intricate details pertaining to the building of this "Holy House." Why is it necessary for scripture to enumerate all the particulars of this project? Hashem instructed Moshe to proceed:

> "…according to all that I show you, the pattern of the Mishkan and the pattern of all its vessels; and so shall you do." (Shemot 25:9).

In describing the actual construction of the *Mishkan* the verse states:

All the work of the Mishkan of the Tent of Meeting was completed; the children of Israel had done [it]; according to all that the Lord had commanded Moshe, so they had done. (Shemot 25:32)

The Torah further states "Moshe beheld their work and indeed they had made it exactly according to all that Hashem commanded Moshe and Moshe blessed them." (Shemot: 49:33). Rashi comments: "He said to them, 'may it be His will to bestow His presence on the work of your Hands.'"

The most important element in erecting the *Mishkan* was absolute dedication to following every instruction of *Hashem*, with no deviation. There is much that we can learn from this. Our task is to serve Hashem in faithfulness without recourse to "strange, unauthorized practices" which He did not mandate.

This is a very relevant message for our times. There are many charms, amulets, incantations and other "*segulot*" which have made inroads in some sections of the religious community. In times of stress there is a temptation to give in to our desire for "lucky charms" and magical "solutions." We must have true faith in Hashem and resist these deviationist practices and serve Him exclusively according to the *mitzvot* He has revealed to us. May we elevate ourselves to serve Hashem in true faithfulness and merit that "His presence should be bestowed on the works of our hands."

The Art of Giving

Parshat Terumah, is the first of four *sedrot* (Torah portions) that deal, in extensive detail, with the construction of the *Mishkan*. The entire nation participated in this communal endeavor. They did so by donating the various materials that were needed for the edifice and its vessels. However, contribution of goods was not the only form of giving. Men and women who were blessed with special artistic and other skills eagerly offered to use them to fashion the very exquisitely contrived objects that were to be housed in the *Mishkan*.

An important lesson can be learned from the generous participation of the nation in building the Tabernacle. The people contributed so much that Moshe announced that no further donations should be given.

The enthusiasm of the people in making contributions reflected a certain level of perfection with regard to their possessions. They did not view wealth as an end in itself. Rather, they saw it as a blessing if it were used to acquire objects of *real*, not imaginary, value. Moreover, the benefit obtained did not have to be purely for oneself. They recognized that their personal existence was bound to that of the nation. Thus, any improvement in the spiritual welfare of the Jewish people would enhance their personal lives as well. This realization precipitated the abundant, "over-giving" which resulted in the unusual call to *halt* the donations.

There were other types of giving as well. Not everyone has sufficient material resources to make contributions. Such a person should not feel inferior, by any means. Material gifts are not necessarily the most precious. One can always give *himself*. Many people possess unique talents that are not being utilized. However, they were of supreme importance in the construction of the *Mishkan*.

While the *Mishkan* no longer exists, the opportunity to contribute one's assets, or one's *self*, is, nevertheless, still available to us. This is so because the Rabbis teach that the Synagogue is a "*Mikdash Me-aht*" (miniature Temple). The reason is because it too fulfills the purpose of the Temple, which is, essentially, to obtain atonement for the Jewish people. This is no longer accomplished through animal sacrifices, which are suspended until the Messianic era. However, the Rabbis have ordained that prayer takes the place of sacrifices.

At first glance this equation seems difficult to comprehend. The sacrifice reminds the person that he is different than an animal and if he lives in a purely instinctual manner it will lead to his destruction. In prayer we praise God and petition Him for our needs. But, how does that serve as a substitute for sacrifices?

In my opinion the key element that prayer and sacrifice have in common is that of humbleness. Both the Temple and the Synagogue demand that a person acknowledge that he is the creation of Hashem who endowed him with a Divine soul which can elevate him to the level of angels. When people acknowledge that their ultimate fate and well-being is in the hands of Hashem, they are worthy of atonement and Divine blessings.

A second similarity is that both the synagogue and the Temple exemplify the element of community. The Rambam teaches that we should always seek to pray at the synagogue with a *minyan*, for the prayers of the community are *always heard*. Even when there are sinners among the congregation, the Holy One blessed be He, does not reject the "prayers of the many" (Mishneh Torah, Laws of Prayer 8:1). One can pray by himself, without a *minyan*, however it is not guaranteed to be received. The primary object of Hashem's providential protection is the *tzibbur* (community) and one must put aside his "rugged individualism" and join the Divinely ordained Jewish community in order to elevate his prayers.

At first glance, it is difficult to see why the Torah devotes so much space to every aspect of the construction of the *Mishkan*, since that institution has been "defunct" for the past two thousand years. However, the Temple lives on in the form of the synagogue. Both serve to unify the Jewish people in recognition of Hashem and acknowledgement of His special relationship with the people who accepted His Torah saying ""We will do everything that Hashem has spoken." (Shemot 19:8).

Once we appreciate the supreme importance of the synagogue in furthering the welfare of the Jewish people, we can understand how it can rightfully be called a *Mikdash Me-aht*. When we give generously of our resources, our talents and our energy, we should do so with the realization that the more we enhance the spiritual life of our people the greater will be our personal satisfaction and reward.

The most important element of one's contribution to the synagogue, like the Temple, is that it be done with a *"leiv shaleim"* (full heart), and with the realization that one is contributing to an endeavor of supreme value.

This attitude is more precious to *Hashem* than the content of one's offering. Even simple acts such as helping to tidy the synagogue, assisting with putting out the *Shabbos Kiddush* or helping with the shul's office work are of the greatest value when motivated by the desire of the individual to *give himself*. May we be inspired to walk in to one of the numerous communal organizations that serve our people and simply declare, "I am ready to help! What do you need me to do?"

The Beautiful People

Parshat Terumah describes in great detail the materials utilized in the construction of the *Mishkan*, its dimensions and the manner of its construction. Gold features prominently among the elements from which the vessels were made. It was not enough, however, to merely cover the outer side of the ark with gold. The verse states:

> And you shall overlay it with pure gold; from inside and from outside you shall overlay it, and you shall make upon it a golden crown all around. (Shemot 25 :11)

According to Rashi, this requirement was fulfilled by constructing three boxes: one of acaccia wood and two of gold. The wooden box, the essence of the ark, was placed inside a gold box and the other gold box was inserted into the wooden box. The ark (the wooden box) was thus covered from within and without with gold. On the surface, this requirement is difficult to understand. Whenever we use gold to enhance the beauty of an object we place it on the outer, visible portion. It would seem wasteful to use precious gold to decorate the inner portion of a vessel which no one will ever see.

I believe that the Torah is teaching us an important lesson. Appearances are important and we should pay careful attention to them. However, we should not be totally consumed with our external image. In our contemporary secular society public perception is regarded as the supreme value. A famous comedian expressed the absurdity of the situation in a skit in which he would say, "it's not important to feel good but to *look good*." Judaism values a pleasant appearance and a good reputation. However, it is equally important to work on our "inner" nature and see to it that the hidden part of man is in line with his outer side. Our character should be "golden" from within and from without.

Rav Soloveitchik said that true holiness consists in how a person behaves when he is away from the public eye, when, in fact, no one is watching. The inner lining of gold teaches that we should pursue goodness for its own sake, and not for public approval. And, of course, the truly wise person knows that "Someone" *is* always watching.

Tetzaveh

Does Clothing "Make the Man?

Pashat Tetzaveh continues to describe the construction of the Mishkan. A great deal of attention is directed at the materials and design of the priestly garments. The *Kohein* (priest) was not permitted to officiate in the Temple in ordinary clothing, however dignified. To do so would be a grave sin and invalidate the service. While it's easy to understand why there would be a "dress code" for something as serious as the Temple service, what's harder to comprehend is the Torah's prescription for the exact materials, measurements and design of the apparel, to the exclusion of the *Kohein*'s personal "taste."

There is a lot we can learn from the Torah's insistence on the sanctity of the *bigdei Kehuna* (priestly garments). For many of us, clothing is more than just a functional necessity. We consider it vitally important to dress "in style," even though our "outdated" apparel is in perfectly adequate condition. In many ways clothing serves as an extension of our image. We all seek to project a certain social persona that reflects how we wish to be perceived by others. Every day we put on our "masks" when we enter into the public domain; we do not want to be seen as we *truly* are. Instead, we invest a lot of money and energy to fashion an appearance we hope will be admired by others.

Our behavior is affected by the clothing we wear. Certain professions require a specific uniform. Pilots, doctors, nurses and policemen must wear their "outfits" while at work. Why does it have to be this way? A skilled professional can perform his craft no matter what he is wearing. Nevertheless, the uniform plays an important psychological role: it reminds him of his professional identity and the seriousness of his mission. While this may not affect his technical skills, it increases the concern and dedication with which he approaches his task.

We can now appreciate the importance of the *bigdei Kehuna*. The verse proclaims: "You shall make holy garments for your brother Aharon, for honor and glory." (Shemot 28:2) Before performing the Temple service, the *Kohein* had to remove his regular clothing, which represents his superficial social image. His priestly garments, however, reflect his true essence, i.e. the Divine soul that is fashioned "in His Image." The uniqueness of man consists in his ability to comprehend the Creator and imitate His ways of truth, justice and compassion. God permits us to perform His Temple service on the condition that we abandon all forms of vanity and focus exclusively on that which is true and eternal.

From this teaching, we learn that we should dress appropriately, but not be excessively preoccupied with "externals." We should affirm that inherent in human dignity is the fact that all people are created in God's image.

Let us appreciate the full significance of one of the fist blessings we recite upon awakening each morning:

> My God, the soul You placed within me is pure. You created and fashioned it and safeguard it within me and will take it from me and restore it to me in the future. As long as the soul is within me I thank You Hashem my God and God of my fathers, Master of all worlds, Lord of all souls. Blessed are You Hashem Who restores the soul to those whose bodies have expired.

May the theme of this blessing be the guiding principle of our temporary sojourn on this earth.

Image and Actuality

Parshat Tetzaveh focuses on those who perform the Temple service. Participation in the activities associated with the Mishkan was not open to all. God chose Aharon and his sons to be the *Kohanim*, and they and their descendants alone were permitted to do the work of the Mishkan. This requirement was so serious that the penalty for a non-*Kohein* who entered the Temple and sought to perform its ritual was death.

Our parsha describes the special garments that were made for the *Kohanim*. The ordinary *Kohein* was outfitted with four garments while the *Kohein Gadol* (Chief Kohein) who performed the special service of Yom Kippur had to don eight pieces of special apparel. These garments were not merely accessories, but were essential to the *Kohein*'s activities. Without them, he was considered lacking in personal holiness and was thus prohibited from performing the service. In a sense, the priestly garments transformed the *Kohein* into an elevated personality fit to minister before Hashem.

On the surface, the great emphasis on the dress code of the *Kohein* seems strange. Judaism does not put much stock in "externals" and outward appearance. This attitude runs counter to the outlook of contemporary society, which adheres to the credo that "clothes make the man." Fashion is a multibillion dollar enterprise; everyone wants to be cool, hip and in style. While there is nothing wrong with wearing nice clothing, we should not get too consumed with how we look.

The clothing we wear reflects not just our subjective tastes, but the type of image we hope to project. Some dress a particular way because they seek to be seen as religious or pious. There is nothing intrinsically wrong with this as long as the person is honest with himself and understands what he is doing — image is not a substitute for reality.

A special type of appearance can confer a false sense of religious security that is not truly warranted. One of the greatest obstacles to *genuine* spiritual growth is an illusory sense of self-righteousness, which the external trappings of religiosity can convey.

Excessive emphasis on the "look" can also be divisive; it might cause some people to look down on others who don't dress the same way. We should never judge a person by these externals. Yet I know of many cases in which people have rejected wonderful *shidduch* (marriage) opportunities because the person did not conform to the desired "dress code." How superficial and mindless, especially for a nation that is supposed to be "wise and discerning."

The garments Moshe was instructed to make for the Priests were special and unique. Hashem said, "You shall make vestments of sanctity for honor and splendor" (Shemot 28:2). These articles were designed by Hashem to reflect the essence of man, his *Tzelem Elokem* (Divine Image). Ordinary clothing reflects man's fantasies and imaginary ideals. They express man's egotistic make up and his yearning for self-glorification. Before entering the Sanctuary to minister before God, the *Kohein* had to remove himself from the world of fantasy and focus on his true essence and purpose. Clothing differentiates man from the animals. Every article that the *Kohein* wore reflected a different aspect of man's mission to acknowledge God and establish a relationship with Him.

Hashem separated the Jews from the nations to serve Him and be a shining example for all. As an example to the nations, we should strive to attain the wisdom of Torah and apply it to all areas of life. It is particularly important that we refrain from being consumed by the passing fads, and desist from mindlessly pursuing the natural inclinations of the heart.

We must be aware of our holiness and cherish it as our most precious gift. We must manifest it in our speech, conduct, dress and preoccupations. Only through an exalted level of wisdom and compassionate deeds can we fulfill our mission to sanctify the name of God in the world.

Never Again

When Parshat Tetzaveh is read before Purim we also read Parshat Zachor, which commands us to "remember and not forget" what Amalek did to us. To properly fulfill this mitzvah we must ask: Who is Amalek, what is his agenda and why is remembering him so vital?

Amalek is the nation that attacked the Jews on the "road when they left Egypt." The Torah does not cite the reasons for this assault. No conflict existed between the two Peoples. Why did the Amalekites venture into the wilderness to initiate unprovoked combat?

We can glean important insight from the strange manner in which Moshe conducted this war. After instructing Yehoshua to select men for battle, Moshe ascended a hill and raised his hands toward heaven. As long as his hands were aloft, the Jews were dominant; but when they were lowered the enemy prevailed. Aharon and Chur then placed a stone beneath Moshe, and while they supported his hands on both sides, Yehoshua defeated the foe.

The commentators ask: What role did the hands of Moshe play in making war? One compelling explanation is that man's excessive fear of other men is rooted in the overestimation of human strength. Genuine courage comes from recognizing the absolute power of Hashem who, alone, determines outcomes.

At this point, the Jews had not fully internalized the idea that "Hashem is a man of war," (Shemot 15:3) which they had witnessed at the Sea of Reeds. When they viewed the upraised hands of Moshe they "subordinated themselves to their Father in Heaven" (Rashi: 17:11) and their strength was renewed. Those who achieve genuine awe of the Creator are liberated from fear of man.

I would like to suggest another dimension to the "hands of Moshe." The war against Amalek was not an ordinary war waged for mundane political reasons. In fact, the real enemy of Amalek was Hashem, and the Jews were a proxy for Him. Amalek struck after the Exodus and the destruction of the Egyptians in the Sea of Reeds: a unique moment of Divine Revelation in the history of mankind. The world trembled in awe of the God of Israel who had demonstrated His supreme might on behalf of His chosen people. Amalek sought to thwart the universal acceptance of Hashem by destroying the Jews. His aim was to replace belief in God with a philosophy that elevated man as the highest being. Moshe raised his hands to demonstrate that the Jews were not fighting for personal reasons but for the sake of God's name. Our national mission is to courageously proclaim, "He is our God, there is no other."

Is Amalek merely a relic of the past or a constantly recurring phenomenon? Rav Chaim Soloveitchik taught that any people who fanatically hate the Jews and seek to destroy them in order to remove Judaism from the world has the status of

Amalek. Haman, who wanted to be worshipped as a god, sought to kill the Jews because Mordechai "would not kneel or bow."

In our time we have seen the worst catastrophes of Jewish history. Hitler's belief in the supremacy of the Aryan race was the underlying cause of his war against the Jews. Rabbi Joseph B. Soloveitchik said that the rabid anti-Semitism of Soviet Russia was an intrinsic outgrowth of its communist ideology, in which deification of the state supplanted God.

We can now appreciate the importance of *remembering Amalek*. During the Holocaust many refused to acknowledge the evidence of the extermination process because they couldn't believe that "humans" were capable of such brutal savagery. Today there are those nations, such as Iran, that deny the Holocaust even while threatening a new one (Heaven forbid). They are perilously close to obtaining the weapons of mass destruction. Let us listen intently to Parshat Zachor and earnestly resolve, "Never Again!"

Ki Tisa

Repeating the Sin of the Golden Calf

Parshat Ki Tisa describes the most egregious sin the Jewish nation could commit: the Golden Calf. We come across many complexities in this story, and it is difficult to fathom how matters could have reached this point. We must start by remembering the central role the crime of idol worship plays in Judaism.

Avraham was selected to be the father of God's chosen people precisely because he discovered the spiritual corruption of idolatry and dedicated his life to liberating humankind from its grip. The Rambam states in the *Guide for the Perplexed*:

> It is the object and centre of the whole Torah to abolish idolatry and utterly uproot it, and to overthrow the opinion that any of the stars could interfere for good or evil in human matters, because it leads to the worship of stars. (Guide 3:37)

The sanctity of the Jewish people lies in the fact that they proclaim the true idea of God and categorically reject any falsification of the pure notion we must have of the Supreme Being. We must be prepared to sacrifice our lives, rather than succumb to the dreadful sin of idolatry.

Indeed, the miracle of Purim came about through Mordechai's defiance of Haman. Mordechai put the entire nation at risk when he refused to bow down to Haman, who had assumed the status of a deity. When we see the lengths Jews such as Mordechai went to in order to avoid bowing to any other being besides Hashem, we are perplexed by the terrible story in our parsha. How could this people, which had been elevated to the status of prophets on Mount Sinai, and who had heard God proclaim, "Thou shalt have no other gods besides Me" (Exodus 20:3), so very soon afterward beseech Aharon:

> "Come! Make us gods that will go before us, because this man Moshe, who brought us up from the land of Egypt, we don't know what has become of him" (Shemot: 32:1).

In studying this matter, we must heed the warning of our sages not to judge someone "until you have been in his place." (Pirkey Avot 2:4) The people who left Egypt were referred to as a "knowledgeable generation." It is easy to be critical of them from the comfortable vantage point of hindsight, but we must reject the temptation. We have a right and an obligation to learn the lessons of historical mistakes, but we must do so with an attitude of humility and refrain from being judgmental.

In seeking a deeper understanding of this sin, we can't help but notice that Aharon allowed himself to become an "accessory" to the crime. While he made a serious mistake, none of the commentators accuse him of aiding or abetting idol worship. All maintain that he would have sacrificed his life rather than violate the second commandment. Indeed, the fact that he was subsequently chosen by God to be the chief *Kohein* confirms that, while his decision was wrong, his motives were pure. What *was* the sin of the Golden Calf?

The great Biblical commentator Ramban asserts that the sin described in our parsha was not that of *overt* idolatry. The Jews were on a high level and did not imagine that a calf crafted from the gold they had worn as ornaments was the Creator of the world. They did not relinquish their belief in the true God who was the Master of the Universe and who had taken them out of Egypt and spoken to them on Mount Sinai.

The failure of Moshe to return at the expected time threw them into a state of severe panic. An inordinate amount of their sense of security was invested in the person of Moshe. After all, he was the vehicle through which all of the miracles had been performed in Egypt and in the wilderness.

The Jewish people lacked confidence that God would continue His providential relationship with them now that Moshe was gone. They erroneously believed that they had to construct something concrete that would become the means through which Hashem would continue to guide them. The purpose of the Golden Calf was not to be an object of worship, but rather to facilitate their ongoing relationship with God.

The people put a great deal of pressure on Aharon to cater to their desire. His purpose, clearly, was to stall for time, for he knew that when Moshe returned, the problem would be eliminated. He asked them to contribute their fine jewelry in the belief that this would slow things down. Unfortunately, he underestimated the people's great urge for an object to guide them.

Proof that Aharon's intention was righteous can be gleaned from his proclamation after the construction of the calf: "Tomorrow we will observe a festival unto Hashem" (Shemot: 32:5). His intention was to use the golden image as an instrument that would retain the people's allegiance to the Creator.

He erred grievously, for the calf opened the emotional floodgates that led the people to idolatry. Rabbi Soloveitchik explains that the difference between the Mishkan and the Golden Calf is that the former was commanded by God, while the latter was a product of man's emotional desires.

We have no right to invent objects of worship. All the articles we use in Divine service must be ordained by Hashem. Only *these* represent true ideas of religious perfection and lead us in the right direction. Those invented by man are the products of his desires and fantasies, masquerading as spiritual impulses. They lead to religious subjectivity in which man deifies the "works of his hands" and worships a deity of his own making.

Today, traditional halakhic Judaism is challenged by many contemporary rabbis and theologians of various denominations, including Orthodoxy, who seek to deviate from the eternal norms of Torah and replace them with a form of worship that Hashem did not command. These are times that try our faith in Hashem, but we must be firm in our commitment to His unchangeable Torah and not yield to those who seek to repeat the sin of the Golden Calf.

Never Despair

No sin is worse than that of *avodah zarah* (idolatry), for it means that we put our faith in "deities" that exist purely in our imagination, and thereby cut ourselves off from a relationship with the true Ruler of the Universe. The Torah reserves its harshest language for the condemnation of idol worship. After the great sin of the Golden Calf, Hashem pronounced this chilling resolution:

> Now leave Me alone, and My anger will be kindled against them so that I will annihilate them, and I will make you into a great nation. (Shemot: 32:10)

Let us consider the significance of this statement. The Jewish people are not unaccustomed to the perils of destruction. We have faced this threat from virtually every tyrant who strode across the pages of history. Pharaoh, Nebuchadnetzar, Haman, the Greeks, the Romans, Hitler and others all sought to crush us. We read in the Haggadah: "In every generation they arise to destroy us but the Holy One, Blessed Be He, saves us from their hands." As long as Hashem is on our side, no force in the world can do us in. However, what we encounter in Ki Tisa is something wholly different and unexpected.

In this parsha, the threat of annihilation comes not from an external enemy, but from *our Protector Himself*! The One Who guards us and guarantees our survival has now turned against us and decreed our demise. What can we do in a situation such as this? How is it possible to avoid paralysis and find a way to prevail?

In this incident, Moshe *Rabbenu* emerged as the greatest Jewish leader of all time. He did not despair but listened carefully to the pronouncement of Hashem when He said: "Now leave me alone that my anger will be kindled against them …" Moshe reasoned, "Why would Hashem tell me to 'leave Him alone' so that He could proceed with His plan to destroy the Jews? It must be that He is hinting to me that everything depends on *me*. He is giving me an opening to contend and plead on behalf of the

Jewish people. There is the possibility that if my efforts are successful I can prevent this tragedy and save the day for *Klal Yisrael* (the Jewish people)."

The greatness of Moshe consisted in his absolute dedication to the nation and his ability to formulate the appropriate plea that would alter the evil decree. Most significantly, he never gave up hope in the possibility of salvaging a seemingly impossible situation. He pleaded with Hashem to rescind the decree for the sake of *His Name*, which would be desecrated by the annihilation of His people, and to "remember the Covenant He had sworn to the patriarchs":

> Moshe pleaded before the Lord, his God, and said: "Why, O Lord, should Your anger be kindled against Your people whom You have brought up from the land of Egypt with great power and with a strong hand? (Shemot: 32:11)
>
> Why should the Egyptians say: 'He brought them out with evil [intent] to kill them in the mountains and to annihilate them from upon the face of the earth'? Retreat from the heat of Your anger and reconsider the evil [intended] for Your people." (Shemot: 32: 11-12)

Moshe's prayer was unique. He did not just pour out his heart and beseech Hashem to have mercy on the Jews. In fact, he said nothing in defense of the people nor seek to mitigate their crime in any way. It seems that he acknowledged their guilt and the justice of Hashem's verdict. Moshe's appeal was based on how the destruction of the Jews would impact the *Egyptians*. The Egyptians would misunderstand it and attribute it to some "defect" in Hashem. They would say that He did not remove the Jews from Egypt in order to benefit His People, but "to slay them in the mountains."

At first glance this argument seems strange. What does it matter *what* the Egyptians think? We must infer that what the Egyptians and, by extension, the other nations think *is* of great importance. Hashem's purpose in performing miracles in Egypt was not only to liberate the Jews. When He informed Moshe of His plan to increase His "signs" and "wonders" in the land He said (Shemot: 7:5): "And *Egypt* will *know* that I am Hashem when I stretch out my Hand over

Egypt and take out the Children of Israel from among them."

It is the will of God that *all* of mankind should recognize Him and live according to His directives. While gentiles are not bound to keep the 613 Commandments, they are obligated to renounce idolatry and abide by the Seven Noachide Laws. The purpose of the Jews is to preserve the Torah and sanctify Hashem's Name in the world not just for ourselves, but for all people.

Thus, Moshe *prayerfully* "argued" to Hashem that "if You destroy the Jews who you extricated from Egypt You will make it virtually impossible to achieve the ultimate goal of their liberation. The annihilation of the Jews would constitute such a devastating *Chillul Hashem* (desecration of the Divine Name) that it would be impossible to rectify. Therefore Hashem, for the sake of Your glory, please rescind the evil decree."

Additionally, Moshe pleaded with Hashem to remember the Covenant He had executed with the *Avot* (Patriarchs).

> Remember Abraham, Isaac, and Israel, Your servants, to whom You swore by Your very Self, and to whom You said: 'I will multiply your seed like the stars of the heavens, and all this land which I said that I would give to your seed, they shall keep it as their possession forever.' (Shemot 32:13)

Rashi explains his petition as follows: "If a chair with three legs can't stand before You at the time of Your anger, how much more so a chair of one leg."

Moshe "argued" that the basis of Jewish identity stems from being descendants of the *Avot* (Patriarchs), who were the ultimate role models in living a life based on knowledge of God and absolute trust in His word. Moshe beseechingly asserted that a new nation descended from only one Father (Moshe), no matter how exalted, would not have the ability to endure when things became very trying. Only the "chair built on three legs" (i.e., the three Patriarchs) could withstand all the trials and tribulations of Jewish history.

Moshe's petition was successful, and Hashem "reverted from the evil He had declared to do to His people." The indefatigable character shown by Moshe *Rabbenu* is the hallmark of a genuine Jewish leader. He never gives up because His faith in Hashem's righteousness is absolute. He knows beyond doubt that Hashem will never abandon His people and this gives him the fortitude to persevere in the most trying and hopeless circumstances.

Another example of this unique leadership quality can be seen in the miracle of Purim. Mordechai's adamant refusal to bow to idolatry triggered Haman's plot of annihilation. The orders had gone out to all the provinces. The Jews were targeted for destruction and the situation seemed hopeless. Yet Mordechai did not despair. He summoned Esther and inspired her to act with the supreme wisdom and courage that the situation demanded. He knew that if the Jews repaired their relationship with Hashem and faced the challenge with the heroism it required, the path to salvation would be open.

We should all be inspired by the examples of Moshe, Mordechai and Esther and all the great leaders of Jewish history. We must never lose faith in the Salvation of Hashem. If we do what is required of us in our time, as our forbears did in theirs, we will certainly merit to witness "light, gladness, joy and honor."

Popularity is No Indicator of Truth

Parshat Ki Tisa begins with the commandment about the proper way to take a census of the Jewish people. The rule is that it is prohibited to count Jews in a straightforward manner. To this day we use indirect methods of counting the number of Jews convened at a given time and place. On the surface the reason for this stricture is difficult to comprehend. Counting seems to be an ordinary, practical necessity devoid of any ethical implications. Why does Judaism take issue with it?

The answer lies in human insecurity. There is a powerful feeling that while an individual is vulnerable, there is strength in numbers. Thus every institute, organization, and society is always preoccupied with "growth" and "expansion." There is an unspoken feeling that bigger is better and the more members you have the more significant you are. Because of this belief, every religion is engaged in proselytizing; they actually believe that numbers mean something, that if more people belong to your religion it increases its validity.

Judaism rejects the notion that popularity is an indicator of truth. To the contrary, people are attracted to that which pleases their emotions, not what is objectively true. Judaism does not seek out, and in fact initially *discourages*, potential converts. Our numbers are miniscule compared to the other "major religions."

Hashem tells us that He did not choose us because of our numbers, for "you are the smallest of all the nations" (Devarim: 7:7). Judaism actually believes that it's very rare for the truth to be popular. Indeed, our father Avraham was called "*Ivri*" (other side) because "all the world was on one side and Avraham was on the other side." The truths he discovered about the existence of God, and the manner in which we should serve Him, were *contrary* to people's religious emotions and remain so to this day.

Judaism does not appeal to our religious feelings but to the Divine soul, the part of us that reasons, understands and comprehends higher truths. It commands us to use our minds in the search for God and to seek to understand His will not as we would like it to be but as He has revealed it to us in His Torah. Our security does not reside in numbers but in the firm conviction, arrived at through diligent study and effort, that *"Moshe emet vetorato emet"* (Moshe is true and his Torah is true).

The counting of people is often utilized by leaders to ascribe importance or validity to an activity or institution, based on the large number of people participating in it. This false notion is antithetical to Judaism's understanding that popularity has little to do with truth.

Today, many leaders formulate their positions on the basis of polls that indicate what is popular with the people. We would be better off if they focused on the intrinsic truth of their policies, regardless of how they will "play with the crowd."

No Compromise

True worship of Hashem must be *exclusive*, for "He is our God, there is *no other*." (Yishiyahu 45:5). It is with a sense of shock and disbelief that we read of the incident of the Golden Calf. We are unable to understand how the Jews could become corrupted so quickly.

It is not our business to judge others. It would be dangerous for us to indulge in a feeling of superiority. We certainly have enough sins on our own plate. Indeed, the Rabbis advise, "Do not judge your friend until you have been in his place." (Ethics of the Fathers 2:4) We should pay careful attention to this sage advice and consider it whenever we are tempted to promote ourselves through the disgrace of others.

At the time of Shemot, the entire world was steeped in idolatry. The Jews had been slaves to Egypt for a few hundred years. The worst aspect of this enslavement was their exposure to the primitive religious doctrines of the Egyptians.

The purpose of the Passover Sacrifice was to cleanse the Jews from pagan beliefs and facilitate their rededication to the worship of the true God, the Creator of the Universe. However, deeply rooted, false religious beliefs are not easily eradicated. In a moment of great fear and danger they can resurface.

We should also remember that the Jews were accompanied by the "mixed multitude," i.e., a group of Egyptians who joined the Jewish people in order to share the benefits they believed would accrue to them. This group was more prone to backsliding and provoked the people to rebellion when the going got tough.

The cause of the sin was the "tardiness" of Moshe. When the people saw that he did not return when expected, they panicked. Their entire sense of security was dependent on the "man Moshe who took us out of Egypt."

> When the people saw that Moshe was late in coming down from the mountain, the people gathered against Aharon, and they said to him: "Come on! Make us gods that will go before us, because this man Moshe, who brought us up from the land of Egypt, we don't know what has become of him." (Shemot 32:1)

The very fact that the Jewish people attributed the Exodus to Moshe and not Hashem revealed something about their mindset. Not that they didn't believe in Hashem, but their relationship to Him was contingent on the "man Moshe." Now that this person was gone a substitute had to be found. This lack of self-confidence and dependency on an intermediary was a carryover from their idolatrous days. All they *really* needed was guidance and instruction, which Aharon was fully equipped to provide. However, they turned to him not for teaching but to satisfy their yearning for an idol.

Aharon's behavior is difficult to comprehend. He clearly understood the grave seriousness of their sinful demand. Why would Aharon, who was at a level of prophecy second only to Moshe, acquiesce in this matter? All the commentators reject the idea that he acted out of fear of the mob, and assert that he would have sacrificed his life to avoid idolatry. Instead, Aharon sought to keep things under control and minimize the extent of the transgression.

He did not want the Jews to stray so far from Hashem that it would be impossible to return. He therefore constructed a Golden Calf that would "replace Moshe" as the vehicle through which Hashem would communicate with them. Aharon thought that the presence of the calf would quell the people's fears and enable them to worship God. Thus he proclaimed, "Tomorrow is a Festival unto Hashem." As the Torah states:

> When Aharon saw [this], he built an altar in front of it, and Aharon proclaimed and said: "Tomorrow shall be a festival to the Lord." (Shemot: 32:5)

Aharon sought to work with the Jews on their level, catering a bit to their emotions, while keeping them firmly committed to Hashem. Despite his great love and concern for the people, we must conclude that he made a serious miscalculation. He did not realize that in the matter of idolatry there can be no compromise, that certain emotions cannot be gratified in "moderation."

There are important lessons for us in this tragic story. Our purpose is not to fashion a god in our image but to direct all of our emotion and energy to following the will of Hashem as He has revealed it to us. We must uproot all traces of idolatry from our hearts and thus find favor with the Creator of the Universe.

Vayakhel

Shabbat and the Mishkan

After discussing the sin of the Golden Calf, Parshat Vayakhel returns to the theme of constructing the *Mishkan*. The verse begins with Moshe gathering the entire people and saying to them:

> "These are the things that the Lord commanded to make." (Shemot: 35:1)

The use of the plural implies that Moshe was giving over more than just one commandment. Indeed, we find that in addition to the instructions about the *Mishkan*, there were exhortations regarding the Shabbat.

Rabbi Joseph B. Soloveitchik points out that, on four separate occasions, the commandment of Shabbat is linked with the *Mishkan*, implying that there is a significant connection between the two. For example, in Parshat Ki Tisa, after describing certain aspects of building the *Mishkan*, the verse states:

> The Lord spoke to Moshe, saying: And you speak to the children of Israel and say: 'However you must keep My Sabbaths! For it is a sign between Me and you for your generations, to know that I, the Lord, make you holy.' (Shemot 31: 12-13)

"*However*, you must keep my Sabbaths." What does the Torah mean by the word "however"? Why is it necessary, in describing the work of the *Mishkan*, to pause and remind us not to forget the Sabbath? What lesson is being communicated here?

The Rabbis derive an important teaching from this unexpected juxtaposition. The term "however" is intended to remind us that, as important and holy as the *Mishkan* is, its construction does not override the observance of the Sabbath. The Torah emphasizes this point because it would not have been unreasonable to believe that the work of constructing the *Mishkan should be* allowed on Shabbat. In fact, the logic of such a proposition is compelling.

On Shabbat we desist from all mundane, "weekday" activities whose purpose is to secure our temporal needs and creature comforts. We refrain from labor as a way to emulate Hashem, whose work of creation was completed on the sixth day. Just as God "rested," that is, desisted from creation on the seventh day, so too must we avoid any creative labor on Shabbat. In doing this, we give testimony to our belief in the Creator, who brought into being everything that exists. One who violates the Sabbath implicitly negates the holiness of the day and denies Creation. Our belief in Hashem is inextricably connected to our conviction that He is the sole Creator and Sustainer of the universe.

Our mandate on Shabbat is to refrain from mundane labor connected to the "struggle for existence," and to redirect our thoughts to the Creator and the proper way to serve Him. Therefore, the Jews might have easily thought that building the *Mishkan* would be permitted on

Shabbat. Clearly, this type of work is in a different category than ordinary labor. The very activity of constructing the *Mishkan* proclaims our belief in Hashem and our responsibility to serve Him.

Note, too, that every aspect of the *Mishkan's* design was dictated by God. Moshe and Aharon were praised because they adhered to every detail of the building plan without instituting the slightest alteration of their own. Thus, in creating the *Mishkan*, every action was an acknowledgment of God and was based on the desire to glorify Him. This type of labor is not the same as that which we do to promote our personal objectives. Why would it *not* be permitted on Shabbat?

We can deduce from the prohibition of building the *Mishkan* on Shabbat that the holiness of this day outranks the holiness of building the Tabernacle. But why? Because there is, indeed, a selfish aspect to the *Mishkan*. Man yearns for a place where God "resides" and from where He "looks out and

173

protects him." The *Mishkan* is fully in line with our ordinary religious needs and desires. People *want* to bring sacrifices. There is in the hearts of most people a sense of guilt and religious insecurity.

In our sober moments when we reflect on our deeds and recognize our transgressions, we have a powerful yearning for God's forgiveness. The message of the *Mishkan* is that there is a ritual we can observe that will secure our pardon. It will cost a few shekels, but that is good; we want to suffer some pain to assuage our guilty conscience. It is a great benefit to be able to purchase a sacrifice, bring it to the Temple, and hand it over to the *Kohein* who will perform the necessary ritual to secure our forgiveness. However, we can't let this attitude distort the entire purpose of Judaism.

Going through the motions of the ritual is not enough. Hashem desires the *heart*. Atonement is secured through our inner transformation, engendered by recognition of sin and determination to improve. That is why the Shabbat is holier than the *Mishkan*. Shabbat does *not* conform to our ordinary emotional desires. A person wants to be free to do whatever he pleases and not be restrained from the "39 types of labor."

To refrain from work and even from discussion of business affairs on Shabbat is a greater expression of holiness than building the *Mishkan*. Dedicating an entire day in which we relinquish our ordinary concerns, and instead contemplate the greatness of the Creator in prayer, Torah study, and festive meals, elevates us to the highest level of human existence. It is only when we proclaim the relevance of Hashem to our lives through the proper observance of Shabbat, that we can truly build a *Mishkan* dedicated to His name.

Hashem is Where You Serve Him

The Torah interrupts the account of the *Mishkan's* construction with the story of the Golden Calf. At first glance this arrangement of the narratives seems strange. The building of the Tabernacle and the sin of the Golden Calf seem to be distinct and unrelated topics. Each one should be covered separately. Yet the Torah did not follow this obvious course. The question is: Why did the Torah introduce the story of the Golden Calf in the middle of the account of the *Mishkan* and its vessels?

The famous Bible commentator known as Sforno has a unique and original explanation. He maintains that the *Mishkan* was not an intrinsic aspect of the Jewish religion. The purpose of the *Mishkan* was to be a place that can be a "habitation" for the *Shechina* (Divine Presence). The verse says, "They shall build for me a Sanctuary and I will dwell among them." (Shemot 25:8) The Sforno explains the verse to mean that Hashem dwells with the people whenever, and wherever, they are following the Torah, as he explains: "...so that I shall dwell in your midst to speak with you and receive the prayers and service of Israel, not as it was before the Golden Calf, as it says 'in every place where I shall cause my Name to be mentioned I will come to you (and bless you)' (Shemot 20:24).

Apparently this commentator holds that there is no necessity for a particular "place" in order to merit the Divine presence. The key is for people to elevate themselves through study, good deeds and heartfelt prayer, all of which will bring us "close" to Hashem. The idea of a "dwelling place" for Hashem should not be taken literally; He does not, after all, have any physical qualities. Rather the idea of God dwelling among us means that He accepts our prayers and provides for our needs through His constant Providence.

We merit the protection and closeness of the Creator by virtue of the perfection we attain through the study of His Torah and observance of His commandments. The location of the place where we turn to Hashem is, in truth, of little consequence. God will respond to us *wherever* we may be, provided that we are pure of heart and mind. If this is so, what is the need for a central Tabernacle where Hashem will "reside among us?"

According to Sforno, the *Mishkan* became necessary as a result of the sin of the Golden Calf. What is it about this transgression that necessitated the construction of the *Mishkan*? I think it has to do with the exalted nature of our belief in God that the Torah requires.

Hashem is an absolutely incorporeal existence and cannot be compared to any of His creations. It's impossible to visualize or depict God in any form, for His Essence is absolutely beyond our comprehension. Man, however, longs for something physical, like a statue, which he can cling to and which creates a certain sense of security. Our concept of God is extremely abstract and does not appeal to our longing for a deity that is conceived in our own imagination. The need to fashion a physical deity in line with our innate emotional needs was at the heart of the sin of the Golden Calf.

Had the Jews resisted this temptation there would have been no need for a *Mishkan*. They would have been on such a high intellectual and spiritual level that they could relate to God *anywhere*. However, now things were different. Hashem gave them a physical structure that would be associated with His name. The vessels utilized in the *Mishkan* were constructed with extreme precision by people of the highest level of artistic skill and advanced Torah knowledge. The Torah records many times that Moshe and Aharon constructed the *Mishkan* in accordance with "all that Hashem had commanded them." (Shemot 39:43) Rashi comments that this comes to teach us that they made no changes of their own.

There is an important lesson here for us. All the objects we use in the service of Hashem express exalted ideas. We should not ascribe magical "powers" to these implements, but seek to understand the teachings they embody. We draw "closer" to Hashem not by being in any particular place but by increasing our knowledge of His will and incorporating it into our behavior. That is what earns Divine favor. May we merit to achieve it.

Of Eternal Value

Parshat Vayakhel describes the success of the plan to obtain the materials and highly skilled labor necessary for building the *Mishkan* through the people's voluntary donations. Apparently, the prospect of contributing in some manner to this awesome enterprise struck a deep chord in the heart of the nation. The verses describe the great generosity that was displayed by the Jews:

> Every man whose heart uplifted him came, and everyone whose spirit inspired him to generosity brought the offering of the Lord for the work of the Tent of Meeting, for all its service, and for the holy garments.

> The men came with the women; every generous hearted person brought bracelets and earrings and rings and buckles, all kinds of golden objects, and every man who waved a waving of gold to the Lord. (Shemot 35: 21-22)

The people were extremely giving of their treasures and skills. The donations were so abundant that a special call went out instructing them not to bring anything more. What can we learn from this phenomenal display of generosity?

The Rabbis say, "Who is wealthy? One who rejoices in his portion." They mean that "wealth" cannot be measured by numbers. We can have millions but be empty, miserable and, yes, *poor*. On the other hand, we can have meager resources and yet feel very content and satisfied. Of crucial importance is our inner state of mind. God has endowed us with talents and abilities as well as with material resources.

We have an innate need to participate in matters that we regard as "important." This stems from the instinctive feeling that life has a larger purpose and that each person has a special mission. Many people have all the creature comforts they can imagine and yet feel unfulfilled. In moments of honesty they realize the shallowness of self-indulgence and long for an opportunity to use their talents and resources for something of eternal value.

The construction of the *Mishkan* was an educational experience for the Jews. Hashem had liberated them from the worst condition: enslavement to base and corrupt people. He had transformed them into a free nation with substantial material wealth. The teaching was: do not remain stagnant and believe that just "breathing free" and luxuriating in the "good life" will make you happy. The freedom granted was an opportunity to develop and use the skills that had been stifled by the Egyptians. The Jews were invited to participate in the construction of the most sublime edifice, the *Mishkan,* which would be the "dwelling place" of Hashem among them. The hearts of the people were inspired with a great sense of generosity. All those with special skills and talents came forth to utilize their abilities, which they recognized had been granted them for just such a purpose.

There is nothing more gratifying than employing our wisdom and skill in advancing a noble cause. Imagine the joy in using your mind to discover the cure for a crippling disease, or to help someone solve a vexing problem, or to establish an institution that will provide tremendous benefit to countless people.

In responding to the call of building the *Mishkan*, the Jews learned that happiness can only come from developing our God-given skills and dedicating them to His service. It is with regard to this type of giving that the Book of Proverbs states:

> The person of kindness (*chesed*) does himself good, but a cruel one troubles his own flesh. (Proverb 11:17)

"The person of *chesed* benefits himself." It's wonderful to have wisdom, skill, and resources. It's even greater to have an opportunity to utilize them for a cause that provides an eternal benefit for humankind and fulfillment for ourselves. Service to the Jewish community and its institutions is not only a great *mitzvah*, it is also the means by which a person can experience deep personal fulfillment and the joyous conviction that life is filled with meaning.

Pekudai

In God's Shadow

Parshat Pekudai provides the final details about the construction of the *Mishkan* and concludes the book of Shemot. The Torah goes out of its way to emphasize the greatness of the people who produced the Tabernacle and its vessels. A high degree of artistic skill was needed to create the holy objects according to God's specific commands. The builders were not only master craftsmen capable of the most exquisite sculpting, they were also men of profound Torah knowledge, with deep insight into the philosophical significance of the structure they were erecting.

A verse at the beginning of the parsha alludes to the wisdom of the artisans:

> Betzalel, son of Uri, son of Hur, of the tribe of Judah, had made all that the Lord had commanded Moshe. (Shemot: 38:22)

The Rabbis comment that the verse should have stated that Betzalel did all that Moshe commanded

185

him. They explain that Betzalel acted according to God's intention, even when Moshe directed him otherwise. Betzalel's insight was so deep that it corresponded to the word of Hashem, even when Moshe gave different instructions.

According to the Rabbis, a disagreement arose when Moshe told Betzalel to fashion the vessels first and *then* to construct the Tabernacle. Betzalel replied that this could not be Hashem's intention, since it is the custom of the world to first build a house and afterward to furnish it.

This story illustrates Betzalel's great intellectual independence. Who would dare disagree with Moshe, who had spoken to Hashem "face to face"? What person would have the nerve to "set him straight" about what he had *really* heard at Sinai? Yet Betzalel is not condemned for disagreeing with Moshe, but is, instead, praised for it.

The Midrash illustrates the true nature of the relationship between a Rebbe (Torah teacher) and his students. The great teacher is the one who inspires and encourages his students to ask questions and learn to think for themselves. There is no greater teacher in Jewish history than *Moshe Rabbenu* (our teacher Moshe), and yet he took no umbrage when Betzalel indicated that Moshe was mistaken in his understanding of Hashem's instructions.

We must ask, however, what exactly was the nature of the disagreement between Betzalel and Moshe? Betzalel's argument, that first you build the house and then arrange its furnishings, seems to make perfect sense. Certainly any ordinary person would understand this, not to mention the greatest prophet of all time. Why would Moshe insist on doing things in a seemingly illogical manner?

There are profound ideas at the root of this "dispute." Moshe maintained that the vessels must be created first, and only then could the Tabernacle be built. He believed that the very manner of constructing the *Mishkan* should convey vital lessons and teachings. He did not want the people to become enthralled with the external edifice. He wanted to communicate that the *Mishkan* had value only insofar as it served to facilitate the Divine Service, which was associated with the vessels. Moshe wanted the Jews to study the ideas and concepts embodied in the *Mishkan's* utensils to achieve this understanding. He thus instructed Betzalel to produce the vessels first, so as to proclaim their supreme importance.

From an abstract philosophical standpoint, Moshe's preferred order of building seems correct. How could anyone argue with the idea that the essence of the *Mishkan* was the special objects used to perform the Divine Service? Betzalel did not disagree with the theory behind Moshe's position. Rather, he argued from the vantage point of *practicality*.

In the natural order of things, people build the house first and then secure the furnishings. Betzalel argued that Moshe should not deviate from the natural order of the world, because that would expose the venture to ridicule. Betzalel recognized that, despite their outer enthusiasm, people also harbor an inner resistance to the service of God. If Moshe acted contrary to people's ordinary perceptions, they would not stop to ponder the deeper significance of his actions. Instead, they would be governed by their initial emotional reaction that "this is not the way things are done."

Moshe was impressed by Betzalel's wisdom. He immediately recognized the astuteness of his argument and acceded to it. He praised Betzalel, saying that his name, which is a compound of two Hebrew words that mean "in the shadow of God," was aptly chosen. Moshe said, "You must have been in God's shadow when He spoke to me, for indeed, what you say is what He actually communicated to me." (Shemot 38:22)

Moshe, the humblest of men, was happy to acknowledge the validity of Betzalel's position. May our love for truth always prevail and enable us to resolve disputes, so we become united in our service of Hashem.

The Courage to *Commit*

Parshat Pekudai is the final section of the Torah dealing with the *Mishkan*. It was an enormous construction project, involving great amounts of building materials, precious metals and highly skilled labor. Upon its completion, Moshe was commanded to set it up and arrange all the vessels in their proper places.

An important part of readying the Tabernacle for use involved an activity known as *Meshicha*: anointing the Tabernacle and all of its vessels with a special oil, thus making them fit for use. The *Kohanim* also had to prepare for service. First they donned the special garments (*bigdei kehuna*), and then they were anointed with the special oil, set aside for that use. The question arises: What was the purpose of the anointing oil and what lesson can we derive from it?

The process of anointing is vital to the successful achievement of the *Mishkan's* objective. The physical properties of the vessels and the skills of those who perform the services are important, but are not enough. Many people attend synagogue or study Torah and perform good deeds, "as the spirit moves them." They tend to these most vital endeavors in a haphazard, sporadic manner. Judaism recognizes the importance of commitment as being essential for maintaining an ongoing involvement in a task.

From a practical standpoint, the *Mishkan* and its vessels, as well as the *Kohanim*, were "ready for action." However, Hashem demanded that they be consecrated with the special anointing oil first. This would serve to dedicate them to the exclusive mission of the Divine service that was to be associated with the *Mishkan*.

Judaism holds that it is not enough to serve Hashem only when we "get the urge." We must recognize that *this* is our purpose and what Hashem created us for. We should dedicate ourselves to the service of God by committing ourselves to Torah study, prayer and good deeds in a conscientious, consistent manner.

Many people have "commitment issues" in various areas of life. The two most prominent ones are interpersonal relationships and religious observance. People fear losing their freedom and autonomy. This is understandable. We shouldn't just jump into things we are not prepared for. However, there comes a time when we must get off the fence and decide. We must have the courage to commit and dedicate ourselves to the most important tasks of life. A great relationship can only be created on the basis of absolute commitment to make it work.

The Jewish people and the Torah way of life have endured despite all the obstacles, because of dedicated, committed souls who *consecrated* their lives to its observance and perpetuation. Let us rededicate and "anoint ourselves" to the Divine mission of being a Kingdom of Priests and a Holy Nation.

Be Strong, Be Strong

Parshat Pekudai completes Shemot, the second book of the Torah. At the conclusion of each of the Five Books of the Torah it is a custom for the congregation to rise and proclaim *"Chazak, Chazak Venischazeik"* (Be strong, be strong and let us be strengthened). This statement is then repeated by the Torah reader. The questions arise: What is the reason for this recitation, why is "Be strong" repeated, and what is the meaning of "and let us be strengthened ?"

The Talmud in *Brachot* (Brachot 32b) states, "Four things need *chizuk* (strengthening): Torah, good deeds, prayer and *derech eretz* (courteous behavior). My understanding of this is that certain activities are contrary to our natural disposition and we therefore become lazy and perfunctory in their performance.

There is nothing in Judaism that is more consequential to religious perfection than the study of Torah. Everything hinges upon diligence in this area. The Rabbis say "An ignoramus cannot be truly pious." (Pirkey Avot 2:6) We must be conscientious in the pursuit of knowledge and expansion of our intellectual horizons.

The public reading of the Torah on Shabbat is for the sake of engaging the entire community in a collective act of *Talmud Torah* (studying of Torah). The need for *chizuk* can be seen in the resistance that many congregants implicitly express by their failure to observe this mitzvah properly. *Halacha* (Jewish law) prohibits any talking or distraction during the Torah reading. Yet in many synagogues it is a great challenge to keep the noise level down so that the recitation can be heard.

Judaism maintains that there is no greater joy than the intense study of Torah. However, it is a unique type of experience, and one that does not come naturally. It requires a great deal of dedicated effort over a long period of time.

Love of Torah is an *acquired* taste. No one becomes a Torah scholar without experiencing a significant amount of frustration and disappointment along the way. Great mental effort, objective analysis and honesty in acknowledging our mistakes are some of the virtues that authentic Torah scholarship requires.

This explains why Torah study is one of the things that require *chizuk*. We must forego the innate desire for instant gratification and be vigilant not to surrender to laziness. This lesson is incorporated into the public reading of the Torah. When we conclude a unit of study (i.e., a Book), we have a natural sense of accomplishment. This is the appropriate moment to express the idea that Torah learning requires strength.

The congregation exhorts the reader (who in this context fulfills the role of teacher) to be strong, i.e., we recognize your great efforts in mastering Torah and urge you to continue. We say "Be strong" twice to convey that he needs be strong both in his ideals and in his behavior. Thus, we say be strong in your study and be equally strong in your effort to live according to the wisdom of Torah. We then say, "*Venischazeik,*" let us be strengthened.

The Torah scholar cannot keep his knowledge to himself. He must be a source of wisdom and inspiration for the entire community. We are praying that he will be strong and successful and that as a result we as a community will share in that strength and elevate our lives by the proper study and practice of Torah.

Glossary of Terms

A

Abarbanel- Isaac ben Judah Abarbanel (1437-1508) was a 15th century Portuguese rabbi, statesman, philosopher, Bible commentator.

Amalek- a tribe that attacked the Jews in the desert, attacking the weak and helpless, and which the Jewish people are commanded to destroy.

Avraham- the Hebrew name of Abraham, the father of the Jewish people.

B

Bamidbar- the Hebrew term for the fourth book of the Torah, known in English as "Numbers."

Bechavruta- learning in partnership with another person in which the Jewish text is explored and analyzed in an active dialectic manner.

Beit Medrash- the study hall of Jewish scholars and students.

Bigdei Kehuna- Literally "clothes of the priests." The priests are required to wear specialized clothes in the performance of their sanctuary rituals. The head priest (kohein gadol) wears 8 specialized pieces of clothing, as opposed to "ordinary" priests who minister with 4 special garments.

Bnei Yisrael– Hebrew for "the Children of Israel" (the Jewish people)

Brisker Derech- A Talmudic methodology developed by Rabbi Chaim Soloveitchik which utilizes an abstract, highly analytic and conceptual approach to traditional Jewish texts.

C

Canaan- the ancient land that was promised to the Jewish people and become the land of Israel.

Chumash- the five books of the Torah.

Chur- the brother of Aaron.

D

Derech- literally this is the Hebrew term for "path", which is often used to describe a teaching and learning methodology utilized in Jewish scholarly activities.

E

Ezekiel- one of the Jewish prophets who lived in the time of the first Temple's destruction and the Babylonian Exile.

G

Guide for the Perplexed- a 12th century Jewish philosophical text written by Moses ben Maimon (Maimonides).

H

Hagaon– a Hebrew term used as an honorary title for a Jewish scholar of exceptional brilliance and importance.

Haggadah - the Jewish text read at the Passover seder which describes the Exodus from Egypt and the rituals performed on Passover to commemorate this event.

Hashem- Literally "the Name" is a reference to God.

Hashkafa- the Hebrew term for a particular worldview and guiding philosophy.

I

Ibn Ezra- An 11th century Spanish commentator on the Torah.

Incorporeality-having no material body or form.

J

Joseph B. Soloveitchik - (February 27, 1903 - April 9, 1993) was a major American Orthodox rabbi, Talmudist, and modern Jewish philosopher. Rabbi Soloveitchik was a scion of the Lithuanian Jewish Soloveitchik rabbinic dynasty. As a *Rosh Yeshiva* of Rabbi in the Isaac Elchanan Theological Seminary at Yeshiva University in New York City, "The Rav", as he came to be known, ordained close to 2,000 rabbis over the course of almost half a century. He served as an advisor, guide, mentor, and role-model for tens of thousands of Jews, both as a Talmudic scholar and as a religious leader. He is regarded as a seminal figure by Modern Orthodox Judaism.

K

Kohanim- the Hebrew term for the priestly group of the Jewish people. They were descendants of the family of Aaron, the brother of Moses and the first High Priest.

L

Levi- this is one of the twelve tribes of Israel. This tribe of Levi had special responsibilities in the services of the Temple and the moving sanctuary in the desert. This was the tribe of Moses and Aaron.

M

Maggid Shiur – one who gives a regular class at a Talmudic academy.

Malbim- Meir Leibush ben Yehiel Michel Wisser (March 7, 1809 – September 18, 1879) was a rabbi, master of Hebrew grammar, and Bible commentator. The name "Malbim" was derived from the Hebrew initials of his name.

Menahel– principal of a Talmudic academy.

Meshicha- a Hebrew term for the anointing of the sanctuary objects with a special oil which needed to be carried out before the vessels could be used.

Midrashim- the plural of the Hebrew term "Midrash" which is the genre of rabbinic literature which contains early interpretations and commentaries on the Written Torah and Oral Torah, as well as non-legalistic rabbinic literature (*aggadah*) and occasionally the Jewish religious laws (*halakha*), which usually form a running commentary on specific passages in the Torah and other books of the Bible.

Mikdash Me-aht- literally "small Temple" - which is a term used for the synagogue, which functions as the place where Jews offers prayers to God and reflect, in a much diminished manner, the Holy Temple of Jerusalem ("Beis HaMikdash" in Hebrew) which before its destruction, was the central place of prayer and sacrificial rites for the Jewish people.

Mishkan- the movable tabernacle that was utilized during the Jewish people's 40 years in the desert. Sacrificial and other religious rites took place in the mishkan carried out by the priests (see kohanim).

Mitzvah– a commandment. 613 Torah commandments were communicated to Moses and the Jewish people at Mount Sinai.

Mitzvot– the plural form of the Hebrew term "mitzvah", which is a Biblical or rabbinic law. (See mitzvah).

Mordechai- a Jewish leader in Persia during the time of the Purim story who was instrumental in the saving of the Jews from annihilation.

Moreinu – the Hebrew term for "our teacher"

Moshe- the Hebrew name of Moses

P
Parshat– the Hebrew for the word "portion of". So the phrase parshat Shemot means the Torah portion of Shemot.

Parsha– the Hebrew term for a Torah portion. The Torah is divided in 54 portions which are read publically in the synagogue on a weekly cycle.

Parshat Zachor- A Torah portion read on the Sabbath before Purim which describes the obligation to remember and avenge Amalek's attack on the Jewish people in the desert.

Pirkey Avot – the Hebrew title of the "Chapters of the Fathers" which is a compilation of the ethical teachings and maxims passed down to the Rabbis, beginning with Moses and onwards. It is part of didactic Jewish ethical Musar literature. Because of its contents, it is also called Ethics of the Fathers. It consists of the Mishnaic tractate of *Avot*, the second-to-last tractate in the order of Nezikin in the Mishnah, plus one additional chapter. Pirkei Avot is unique in that it is the only tractate of the Mishnah dealing *solely* with ethical and moral principles; there is little or no halacha (laws) found in Pirkei Avot.

R

Rambam- Rabbi Moses ben Maimon also known as Maimonides, was a 12th century Spanish Torah commentator on the Mishna and author of the monumental work, the Mishnah Torah which,for the first time, codified all of Jewish law. He was also a major Jewish philosopher of the rationalist school.

Ramban- Rabbi Moses ben Nachman, also known as Nachmanides, was a 13th century Spanish commentator on the Torah, the Bible and the Talmud.

Rashi- Rabbi Shlomo Yitzchaki, an 11th century French commentator on the Torah, Bible and Talmud.

Reaction formation- A psychological defense mechanism by which a repressed impulse is expressed in an opposite behavior.

Roshei Yeshiva- plural of "Rosh Yeshiva", the head of a Talmudic academy.

K

Kohein Gadol- the chief of the priests who officiated at the Yom Kippur service.

S

Samson Raphael Hirsch- was a 19th century German Orthodox rabbi best known as the intellectual founder of the *Torah im Derech Eretz* school of contemporary Orthodox Judaism. He has had a considerable influence on the development of Orthodox Judaism.

Schechina- a Hebrew word meaning "dwelling" or "settling" and denotes the dwelling or settling of the divine presence of God.

Segulot- these are protective/benevolent charms or rituals in Kabbalistic and Talmudic tradition.

Shemot- The Hebrew title for the second book of the Torah known in English as "Exodus."

Shiurim- the Hebrew term for classes in Jewish subjects.

Sugya- the term used to delineate an area of study or a type of subject matter.

T

Talmud- the Talmud is the Jewish Oral Law which accompanies the Written Law of the five books of the Chumash. The Talmud consists of 63 tractates, and in standard print is over 6,200 pages long. It is written in Tannaitic Hebrew and Jewish Babylonian Aramaic and contains the teachings and opinions of thousands of rabbis (dating from before the Common Era through the fifth century CE) covering a broad variety of subjects, including Halakha (law), Jewish ethics, philosophy, customs, history, lore and many other topics. The Talmud is the basis for all codes of Jewish law, and is widely quoted in rabbinic literature.

Talmid- the Hebrew term for "student."

Talmidim –the Hebrew term for "students."

Tanach- the Hebrew term for the Jewish Bible.

Teshuva- the Hebrew term for "repentance".

V

Vayikra- the Hebrew term for the third book of the Torah, known in English as Leviticus.

Y

Yaakov- the Hebrew name for Jacob.

Yosef- the Hebrew name for Joseph.

Yehoshua- the Hebrew name of Joshua.

Made in the USA
Columbia, SC
21 April 2021